The Battle of the Crater

CIVIL WAR CAMPAIGNS AND COMMANDERS SERIES

Under the General Editorship of Grady McWhiney

PUBLISHED

Battle in the Wilderness: Grant Meets Lee by Grady McWhiney
Death in September: The Antietam Campaign
        by Perry D. Jamieson
Texans in the Confederate Cavalry by Anne J. Bailey
Sam Bell Maxey and the Confederate Indians by John C. Waugh
The Saltville Massacre by Thomas D. Mays
General James Longstreet in the West: A Monumental Failure
        by Judith Lee Hallock
The Battle of the Crater by Jeff Kinard

FORTHCOMING

Cottonclads! The Battle of Galveston and the Defense of the
        Texas Coast by Donald S. Frazier
A Deep, Steady Thunder: The Battle of Chickamauga
        by Steven E. Woodworth
The Texas Overland Expedition by Richard Lowe
Raphael Semmes and the Alabama by Spencer C. Tucker

The Battle of the Crater

Jeff Kinard

Under the General Editorship of Grady McWhiney

RYAN PLACE PUBLISHERS
FORT WORTH

Cataloging-in-Publication Data

Kinard, Jeff, 1954—
The Battle of the Crater / Jeff Kinard.
     p. cm. — (Civil War campaigns and commanders)
     Includes bibliographical references and index.
     ISBN 1-886661-06-5 (pbk.)

     1. Petersburg Crater, Battle of, Va., 1864. I. Title. II. Series.
     E476.93.K56 1995
     973.7'37—dc20   95–33310
                                                     CIP

2730 Fifth Avenue
Fort Worth, Texas 76110

ISBN 1-886661-06-5
10 9 8 7 6 5 4 3 2 1

Book Designed by Rosenbohm Design Group

All inquiries regarding volume purchases of this book should be
addressed to Ryan Place Publishers, Inc., 2525 Arapahoe Avenue,
Suite E4-231, Boulder, CO 80302-6720.

A Note on the Series

Few segments of America's past excite more interest than Civil War battles and leaders. This ongoing series of brief, lively, and authoritative books–Civil War Campaigns and Commanders–salutes this passion with inexpensive and accurate accounts that are readable in a sitting. Each volume, separate and complete in itself, nevertheless conveys the agony, glory, death, and wreckage that defined America's greatest tragedy.

In this series, designed for Civil War enthusiasts as well as the newly recruited, emphasis is on telling good stories. Photographs and biographical sketches enhance the narrative of each book, and maps depict events as they happened. Sound history is meshed with the dramatic in a format that is just lengthy enough to inform and yet satisfy.

Grady McWhiney
General Editor

CONTENTS

CAMPAIGNS AND COMMANDERS SERIES

Map Key

Geography

	Trees
	Marsh
	Fields
	Strategic Elevations
	Rivers
	Tactical Elevations
)|(	Fords
	Orchards
— — — — —	Political Boundaries

Human Construction

⊰)(	Bridges
+++++++++	Railroads
	Tactical Towns
● ○	Strategic Towns
□ ■	Buildings
✝	Church
✕	Roads

Military

▬ ▬	Union Infantry
▭ ▭	Confederate Infantry
▱ ▨	Cavalry
⼁⼁⼁	Artillery
	Headquarters
△ △△ △ △△ △ △ △	Encampments
⟡	Fortifications
	Permanant Works
	Hasty Works
	Obstructions
☆ ✦ ✦ ✂	Engagements
	Warships
◀▬	Gunboats
	Casemate Ironclad
◀●▬	Monitor
↺ ⇨	Tactical Movements
➝	Strategic Movements

*Maps by
Donald S. Frazier, PhD.
Abilene, Texas*

MAPS

PHOTOGRAPHS

The brief biographies accompanying the photographs were written by Grady McWhiney and David Coffey.

The Battle of the Crater

1
THE KEY TO RICHMOND

By the summer of 1864, Richmond, Virginia, was a city under siege. As Union General Ulysses S. Grant's powerful Army of the Potomac tightened its grip on the Confederate capital, General Robert E. Lee rushed the battered remnants of his Army of Northern Virginia into the city's outer defenses. Weakened by three years of constant fighting, Lee's army was still dangerous; just weeks earlier it had inflicted horrendous losses on the Federals in the battles of the Wilderness and Spottsylvania. On June 3, east of Richmond near a tavern known as Cold Harbor, Grant's troops suffered 7,000 casualties in a matter of minutes while assaulting the Rebel lines. Still, Grant's resources seemed endless while Lee's were reduced to a trickle along a tenuous lifeline to his south.

Nestled on the bank of the Appomattox River twenty-three miles south of Richmond, Petersburg was the key to the Confederate capital's survival. Nine wagon roads and five railroad connections radiating from the city marked it as a strategic transportation hub. Two eastern tracks, the eight-mile route to City Point and the Norfolk line, were cut by Grant's forces in June, but three vital lines remained open. The Southside Railroad to Burkesville and Lynchburg and the Weldon and Wilmington Railroad to North Carolina still connected the city to major supply sources in the lower South. These lines poured food, supplies, and troops into the city where they were transferred to the Richmond-Petersburg Railroad and on to Richmond and Lee's Army of Northern Virginia. Should these last links be severed, Lee's army would starve.

Petersburg was second to Richmond as Virginia's largest city. Of its peacetime population of 17,266, 5,680 were slaves, and 3,164 were free blacks, many of whom were skilled workers in the city's thriving economy. Revenue from Petersburg's

Burial detail at Cold Harbor

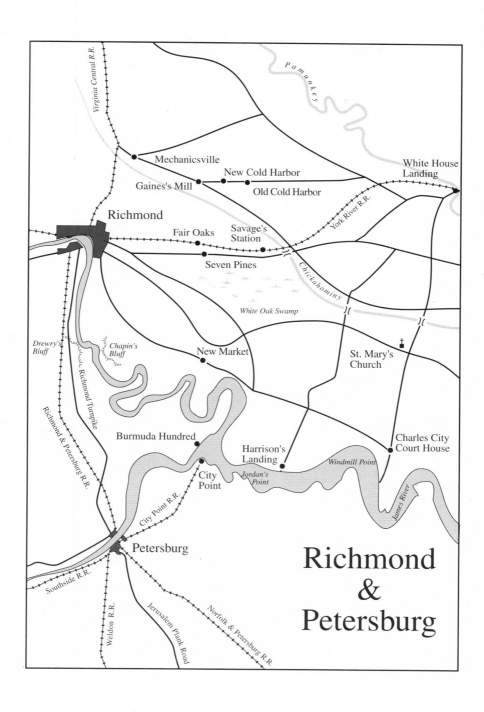

Richmond
&
Petersburg

twenty tobacco factories and six cotton mills allowed its citizens to enjoy paved, gas-lit streets and a modern water system. Other urban amenities included two newspapers, six banks, and a skyline graced with the steeples of thirteen churches. As the war progressed, the city's population swelled with refugees and troops on their way to the front.

As early as 1863, Mrs. Roger A. Pryor recalled, "Petersburg was already virtually in a state of siege. Not a tithe of the food needed for its army of refugees could be brought into the city."

View of Petersburg

Wartime inflation and shortages were rampant. Still, military hospitals were established to handle the flood of sick and wounded from the Richmond defenses, and a Home Guard was organized. Three years of war had stripped the city of its able, military-age men. The Home Guard, under former Virginia Governor Henry Wise, was composed of barely a thousand teenage boys and men in their fifties and sixties. It was these troops, armed with obsolete muskets, who defended Petersburg in the first battles of what would become the

longest siege ever endured by an American city.

Petersburg's defenders owed much of their salvation to a line of massive earthen forts east of the city known as the Dimmock Line. Begun in the summer of 1862 under the direction of Captain Charles H. Dimmock, the line was a masterpiece of military engineering. Anchored on the Appomattox, northeast of Petersburg, the fortifications extended in a ten-mile arc to a point on the river below the town. Its fifty-five artillery emplacements were connected by a series of trenches fronted with cleared fire zones and infantry obstacles including abatis—tangles of felled trees, and chevaux-de-frise—logs projecting sharpened stakes. As the siege progressed, the troops, aided by local slaves, extended and improved their fortifications. As protection from mortar and other artillery fire, they constructed bewildering mazes of "bombproofs." These were log- and earth-covered caves connected by covered ways

Confederate cannon at Petersburg

or trenches through which the men could pass without exposing themselves to enemy sharpshooters.

Stopped by these formidable obstacles, the Federals also began to dig. Within a matter of weeks, a double line of opposing trenches stretched fifty-one miles from north of Richmond to south of Petersburg.

As the sun baked the torn earth around Petersburg, the men settled into the grim routine of trench life. Sweating and covered with layers of thick dust, they alternated between improving their fieldworks, picket duty, and fatigue details.

Defensive works at Fort Sedgewick

Death, as always, remained a daily occurrence. Disease, artillery fire, and sharpshooters claimed a steady quota of victims.

To relieve boredom, both sides often baited the enemy's sharpshooters. Squatting out of sight in a forward trench or rifle pit, the men would raise a hat above the parapet on a ramrod. The resulting well-ventilated headgear would often decide the outcome of wagers, but most graphically acted as a strong reminder to keep one's head down. Other diversions included cards, checkers, and drinking.

In addition to the dull existence and discomforts inherent to trench life, Southern troops also had to deal with constant shortages. Rations, when available, were usually a monotonous affair of raw fatback, hardtack or corn bread, and, on occasion, coffee. To relieve both the tedium and ammunition shortages, men from Bushrod Johnson's Division scrounged around their trenches for spent Union bullets and unexploded artillery shells. J. A. Reamy, a private in the 34th Virginia, turned in 1,567 bullets and four artillery projectiles in a single day. The salvaged Union ordnance was duly remanufactured in Richmond armories and returned to the troops as new, Confederate ammunition.

Cheváux-de-frise

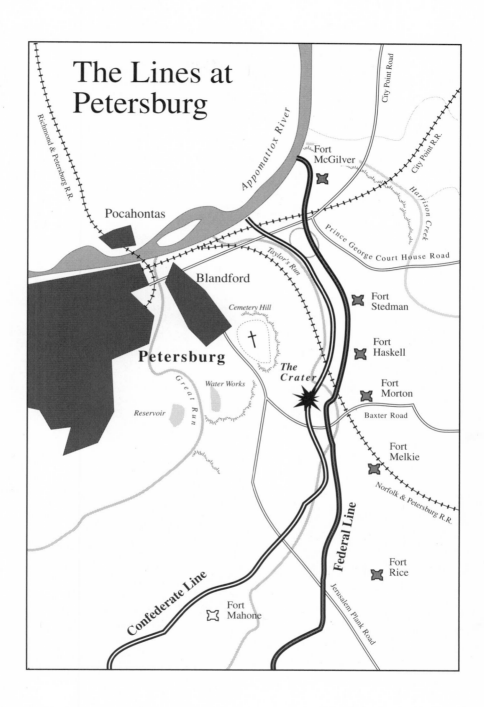

The Lines at Petersburg

City Point Road

Richmond & Petersburg R.R.

Appomattox River

Fort McGilver

City Point R.R.

Harrison Creek

Pocahontas

Prince George Court House Road

Taylor's Run

Blandford

Cemetery Hill

Fort Stedman

Petersburg

Fort Haskell

Great Run

Water Works

The Crater

Fort Morton

Reservoir

Baxter Road

Fort Melkie

Norfolk & Petersburg R.R.

Federal Line

Confederate Line

Fort Rice

Jerusalem Plank Road

Fort Mahone

Federal troops, entrenched as little as four hundred feet away, shared much the same existence as their Rebel opponents. Although infinitely better supplied by their massive depot at City Point, they too endured the loneliness and miseries of trench life. Alternating in shifts of four days in the forward lines and two days in the rear, they were constantly exposed to the elements. The searing heat of the summer sun

Federal sharpshooters at work in front of Petersburg

on their lice-infested, woolen uniforms or the occasional rain and mud were frequent companions. Amid the squalor, Union divisions typically lost between fifteen and twenty men a day, usually from head wounds. As the summer dragged on, the men's thoughts became ever more concerned with some decisive move that would end the war.

2
THE PLAN

A mining engineer before the war, Henry Pleasants was a lieutenant colonel in the trenches of the Union Ninth Corps southeast of Petersburg. His regiment, the 48th Pennsylvania Volunteers, were for the most part coal miners from Schuylkill County in the eastern region of the state. For weeks, Pleasants and his men had endured deadly, point-blank shelling and sniping from two regiments of South Carolinians in a strong earthen redoubt little more than a hundred yards away.

Elliott's Salient, as the fortress was called, occupied a strategic position in the Confederates' last line of defense. Only a half-mile from Petersburg's outskirts, the four-gun stronghold also protected a stretch of the important Jerusalem Plank Road just 500 yards to the rear. Directly behind the salient, Confederate engineers had constructed an observation trench protected by a parapet on Cemetery Hill, a ridge that commanded the surrounding countryside. As further protection, batteries of Coehorn mortars and twelve pounder Napoleon field guns could be brought to bear on the area from three angles. To Henry Pleasants, the formidable Elliott's Salient was the only obstacle barring the Federal army from marching into Petersburg.

Pleasants was not the only man in the Pennsylvanians' trenches mulling over the problem. In a discussion with some of his men, one of the miners offered, "We could blow that damned fort out of existence if we could run a mine shaft under it." The idea instantly appealed to the inventive Pleasants. He was sure that given proper support, his men could tunnel under the fort, place and detonate explosive charges beneath it, and shorten the war.

Henry Pleasants: born South America 1833; raised in Pennsylvania, he became a railroad engineer; turning his attention to mining, he worked in Pennsylvania's coal region, developing new techniques in deep shaft mining; with the outbreak of the Civil War he joined the 6th Pennsylvania Infantry as a 2d lieutenant, but the regiment mustered out in July 1861; the following month Pleasants joined the 48th Pennsylvania Infantry as a captain; he participated in General Ambrose Burnside's North Carolina Expedition, at Second Bull Run,

and Antietam; elevated to lieutenant colonel in September 1862, he fought at Fredericksburg that December; on detached duty for several months, he rejoined his regiment in the spring of 1864; with Army of the Potomac in Virginia, he fought in the Wilderness, at Spotsylvania Courthouse, and throughout General U.S. Grant's Overland Campaign; at Petersburg some soldiers of his regiment advanced the idea of digging a mine shaft to be exploded under the Confederate line; after Pleasants secured authorization, members of the 48th Pennsylvania completed the shaft that was exploded on 30 July 1864, resulting in the Battle of the Crater; despite the disastrous outcome, Pleasants was brevetted brigadier general of volunteers for his efforts in constructing the mine; he mustered out with his regiment in December 1864; following the war he resumed mine engineering in Pennsylvania; later involved in law enforcement, he was active in suppressing the "Molly Maguires." Colonel Pleasants died in 1880.

On June 24, after ironing out a few details, Pleasants presented the plan to his superior, General Robert B. Potter, commander of the Second Division. Impressed, Potter passed the plan up to the Ninth Corps commander, General Ambrose Burnside. Always open to novel ideas, Burnside wholeheartedly endorsed Pleasants's proposal and within hours rode to General George G. Meade's headquarters for final approval.

Unfortunately, Meade had little regard for Burnside's judg-

Robert B. Potter: born New York 1829; attended Union College at Schenectady, New York, but did not graduate; he studied law and was admitted to the bar, practicing in New York City until the outbreak of the Civil War; enlisting as a private in the New York militia, he was soon elevated to lieutenant; in October 1861 he was commissioned a major in the 51st New York Infantry and promoted to lieutenant

colonel a month later; during General Ambrose Burnside's North Carolina Expedition Potter was conspicuously engaged at Roanoke Island and was wounded at New Bern in March 1862; he fought during the Second Bull Run Campaign and was promoted to colonel in September 1862; at Antietam, he managed to get his troops over Burnside's Bridge after others had repeatedly failed; after fighting at Fredericksburg in December 1862, he was transferred to the Western Theater with the Ninth Corps; promoted to brigadier general of volunteers in March 1863, he commanded a division in the Vicksburg Campaign and directed the Ninth Corps at Knoxville; the corps returned to the Eastern Theater in the spring of 1864, where Potter headed a division in the Overland Campaign; during the Siege of Petersburg in July 1864, the 48th Pennsylvania of Potter's Division constructed the mine that was exploded beneath the Confederate lines; in the ensuing assault on the Crater Potter was the only division commander in Burnside's Corps present with his troops on the field, earning the brevet to major general of volunteers; he was severely wounded in the final assault on Petersburg in April 1865; promoted to the full rank of major general of volunteers in September 1865, he was mustered out the following January; after the war he worked in the railroad business and spent four years in England before settling in Newport, Rhode Island. General Potter died at Newport in 1887.

Ambrose Everett Burnside: born Indiana 1824; apprenticed to a tailor and worked in a shop until friends of his father, an Indiana legislator, secured him an appointment to the U.S. Military Academy, where he graduated eighteenth in the class of 1847; appointed 2d lieutenant in 3rd Artillery in 1847, but saw little service in Mexico; promoted to 1st lieutenant in 1851; married Mary Richmond Bishop of Rhode Island in 1852 and resigned from army a year later to manufacture a breech-loading rifle he invented; company went bankrupt in 1857; major general in the Rhode Island militia and treasurer of the Illinois Central Railroad before the Civil War; in 1861 organized and became colonel of 1st Rhode Island Infantry, which was among the earliest regiments to reach Washington; became friend of President Lincoln and received promotion to brigadier general of volunteers in August 1861 after commanding a brigade at the Battle of Bull Run; in 1862 commanded a successful operation along the North Carolina Coast; commissioned a major general of volunteers and received awards and thanks from various states; at Sharpsburg he wasted too much time crossing Antietam Creek and attacking the Confederate right; after twice declining command

of the Army of the Potomac, he finally accepted, although he considered himself incompetent and proved himself correct by crossing the Rappahannock River in December 1862 and making a disastrous attack on the awaiting Confederate army at Fredericksburg; "I ought to retire to private life," Burnside informed President Lincoln, who after relieving him of command in the East assigned him to command the Department of the Ohio; at Lincoln's urging, he advanced into East Tennessee and in November 1863 repulsed an assault on Knoxville by Confederates under James Longstreet; Burnside and his Ninth Corps returned to the East in 1864 to serve under Grant from the Wilderness to Petersburg; blamed by General George Meade for the Union failure at the Crater, Burnside shortly thereafter went on leave and never returned to duty; in 1865 he resigned his commission; after the war he became president of various railroad and other companies; elected governor of Rhode Island in 1866 and reelected in 1867 and 1868; elected to U.S. Senate from Rhode Island in 1874, where he served until his death at Bristol, Rhode Island, in 1881.

ment. Once Burnside's subordinate, Meade had risen to command the Army of the Potomac following Burnside's disastrous defeat at Fredericksburg. Accompanied by his Chief of Engineers, Major James C. Duane, Meade listened impatiently to Burnside's overly detailed proposition. Both men were aware that a similar plan had failed miserably during the siege of Vicksburg the previous year at the cost of many Federal lives. Now, Pleasants's mine would require nearly three times the blasting powder of the Vicksburg project and the tunnel itself would be over ten times its length.

To a trained engineer, the logistical problems were obviously insurmountable. Despite Duane's dismissal of the whole scheme as "claptrap and nonsense," Meade at last conde-

Digging the tunnel

scended to refer the proposal up the chain of command to his superior, General Ulysses S. Grant. Though less than enthusiastic, Grant gave his approval, mainly to keep his bored troops occupied.

In the meantime, Pleasants had already begun his tunnel. At noon on June 25, his men began excavating the mine in a ravine a hundred feet behind their front line. Out of sight of the Confederate lookouts, Pleasants's foreman, twenty-eight-year-old Sergeant Henry Reese, made camp next to the entrance and organized the men into three-hour shifts working round the clock.

"I found it impossible to get any assistance from anybody, I had to do all the work myself." That was how Henry Pleasants accurately summed up the situation he and his men faced. Although Pleasants had been promised complete cooperation, Major Duane seemed to take satisfaction in denying the miners even the most rudimentary equipment. As Major Oliver Bobbyshell described the situation: "No tools, no planks, no nails, no wheelbarrows. Army picks were shortened and made smaller for mining purposes. Hickory sticks were fastened to cracker boxes so as to make handbarrows, to convey the material excavated to a place where it could be piled outside the mine." As their supply of scrap timber for bracing the mine dwindled, the men scoured the countryside for suitable lumber. After stripping a nearby bridge of its planking, they discovered an abandoned sawmill behind their lines and put it into operation, laboriously hauling the boards nearly six miles back to the mine.

Despite the many setbacks, the men were able to excavate as much as forty or fifty feet a day. The cramped interior of the tunnel was described by one of the miners as "about four and a half feet high, nearly as many feet wide at the bottom and two feet wide at the top." Working by candlelight, one man would dig while, as the mine progressed, an ever-increasing number of workers would haul the excavated clay and other material to the entrance. Eventually, nearly 400 men were involved, almost the entire enlisted strength of Pleasants's regiment. At the end of each three-hour shift, Sergeant Reese would reward each of the bone-weary men with "2 good drinks of whiskey" from a tin cup. Some of the men, however, managed to save enough of their ration to get drunk, and "made fools of themselves," so the practice soon stopped.

On July 2, disaster struck. After a week of steady digging, the men reached what Pleasants described as "extremely wet ground." With water and mud pouring down from between the boards overhead, the miners worked desperately in the claustrophobic space to brace the sagging ceiling. As candles sputtered out, the waterlogged timbers gave way and the roof collapsed. Miraculously, no one was seriously injured. Soon after the soaked Pennsylvanians splashed to safety, Sergeant Reese had them back at work, removing the wreckage and reinforcing the weakened section. The digging continued.

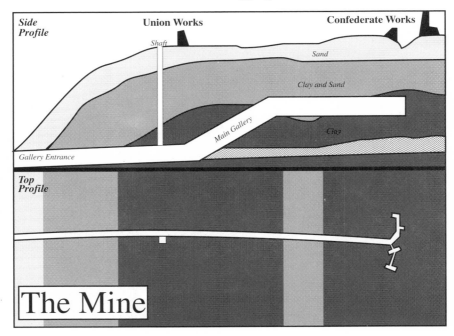

The mine's steady progress created other problems as well. One of the most serious was what to do with the material excavated from the tunnel—according to Pleasants, an incredible 18,000 cubic feet in all. As the work proceeded, the rapidly increasing mounds of freshly dug clay stood in sharp contrast to the sunbaked, dusty soil near the tunnel's entrance. In order to conceal the telltale debris from Confederate lookouts, Pleasants ordered the men to remove it far behind the lines where they took the added precaution of covering it with underbrush. Also, about halfway into the project, the Pennsylvanians encountered a deposit of marl, a dense, putty-like soil that was extremely difficult to dig through. Pleasants reported later that "to obviate it the range of the tunnel was carved upward, so that the latter half was several feet higher than at the entrance." It was, however, the ventilation of the mine that would prove to be the true test of Pleasants' abilities. Military engineering experience held that a tunnel such

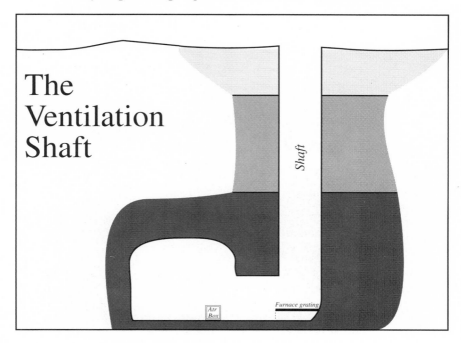

The Ventilation Shaft

Shaft

Air Box

Furnace grating

as the Pennsylvanians' could not be ventilated past 400 feet, but to reach the Confederate stronghold, the tunnel had to extend over 500 feet. From the beginning, Major Duane, along with Meade's other engineers, had scathingly dismissed the project primarily because of the ventilation problem. Still, although educated at West Point, which provided the best engineering instruction in the country, Duane did not reckon on the resourcefulness of a man who had honed his engineering skills in Pennsylvania's coal fields. Pleasants instructed his men to build an eight-inch square wooden duct along a corner of the shaft, which they extended as they deepened the mine. About one hundred feet from the mouth of the tunnel they bored a shaft twenty-two feet to the surface that opened just behind their front trenches. At the bottom of the shaft they constructed a small furnace where they kept a fire constantly burning. They finally rigged an airtight burlap curtain across the mine's entrance. In effect, Pleasants converted the entire tunnel into a giant flue that drew the stale air up through the shaft allowing fresh air to enter through the duct where the miners were digging.

Aware that the Confederates now knew of the mine's existence, Burnside ordered decoy fires to be lit along his front to mask the tunnel's exhaust smoke plume.

Just a few yards away, the Confederates were also busy. Rumors had persisted for weeks that the Federals were mining, but Rebel observers could not pin down the operation's exact location. Finally, on June 30, General E. Porter Alexander, chief of ordnance for the Army of Northern Virginia, noticed something peculiar. The ever-present sharpshooter activity was much heavier in front of Elliott's Salient than anywhere else along the line. Convinced he had discovered the mine's location, Alexander, in his hurry to reach Lee's headquarters with the news, was shot through the hand by one of these same sharpshooters as he crossed an exposed area between the trenches. Before returning home to recuperate,

Alexander reported his suspicions to Lee's aide, Colonel Charles Venable, who passed the information on to the general.

Alexander's deduction confirmed his fellow officers' fears. Captain Hugh Douglas had already begun counter-mining operations in and around the salient with his newly arrived engineer company. He was soon reinforced by levies of an additional 160 men donated by nervous local commanders. Douglas soon had a series of ten-foot vertical shafts radiating side-galleries in various directions along the Confederate front.

A subterranean cat-and-mouse game ensued as the men strained their ears for the sound of the other's picks deep in the Virginia clay. One Rebel counter-mine was so close to the tunnel that there is the possibility that Pleasants and Douglas

Confederate counter-mine

were within ten feet of one another as they supervised their operations. Although the threat of discovery forced Pleasants to slow the progress of the mine, Douglas's efforts failed and the Pennsylvanians continued their digging.

As the project neared completion, Pleasants realized that "the great difficulty to surmount was to ascertain the exact distance from the entrance of the mine to the enemy's works, and the course of these works." The most effective device for making such necessary calculations was a surveying instrument known as a theodolite. Major Duane, at Meade's headquarters, had one of the latest models of theodolite but, true to form, refused to loan it to the determined Pennsylvanians. Knowing that Pleasants was in desperate need of the instrument, Burnside asked friends in Washington to send him a functional but obsolete model. As an aide wiggled a hat on a ramrod to draw sniper fire, Pleasants, "within 133 yards of the enemy's line of sharpshooters," repeatedly popped his head over the rim of a bullet-churned trench to take his readings. Finally, on July 17, he calculated the tunnel, at 510.8 feet, to be directly under the Confederate stronghold.

The 48th Pennsylvania had succeeded in digging the longest military tunnel ever attempted. The men next began to dig two side-galleries which extended a little less than forty feet in each direction to the left and right of the main gallery. Off from each side-gallery the men excavated four magazines for the powder charges. The final process had to be carried out with extreme caution as the Confederates were directly overhead and on the alert for suspicious subterranean sounds. On July 17, alarmed by an unusual amount of activity in the gun emplacements above, the miners quickly dropped their picks. Pleasants again hurried into the gallery, but after a few hours of tense listening, decided it was merely the Confederate gunners reinforcing their position. He ordered the mining to continue the next day. Pleasants's men even resorted to measuring and constructing the wooden bracing outside of the tunnel, disassembling it and then reassembling it inside, without hammers, to reduce noise. Again, on the eighteenth, the men in the right gallery heard digging noises directly overhead, and unsure whether it was a counter-mine or merely normal construction, angled the mine around the area.

By six o'clock in the evening, July 23, the mine was complete and ready to be charged with explosives. The merit of the Pennsylvanians' accomplishment was, not surprisingly, lost upon the officers at Meade's headquarters. Major Duane's men delivered only four of the six tons of blasting powder Pleasants requested, and rather than waterproof "safety fuse," he sent regular blasting fuse scraps requiring skilled splicing.

Nevertheless, on the afternoon of July 27, the miners loaded the highly explosive twenty-five-pound powder kegs into burlap sacks and ran the harrowing gauntlet of rifle and mortar fire from the storage area to the mine entrance. By 6 P.M., July 28, the men had finished packing the 320 powder kegs in

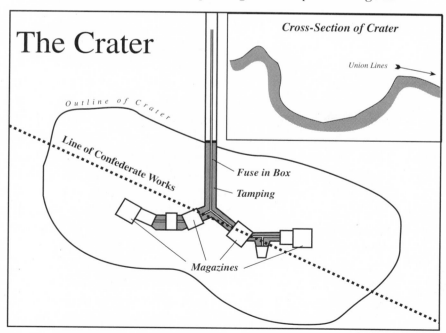

The Crater

Cross-Section of Crater

Union Lines

Outline of Crater

Line of Confederate Works

Fuse in Box

Tamping

Magazines

the magazines under the doomed fort. After tamping the charges with hundreds of sandbags to direct the blast upward rather than allow it to funnel backward down the tunnel into the Union trenches, the men began preparing the fuses.

The tension in the mine was palpable as the miners readied the fuses. As the men poured the loose powder into the open wooden trough that connected the eight magazines, their only light was from lanterns and candles which, if tipped over, would end their lives in one spectacular flash. They next connected the powder-filled trough to three lengths of fuse that ran ninety-eight feet toward the main gallery's entrance. The men were old hands at such work, however, and the fuse laying went without a hitch. On July 28, Pleasants hurriedly reported to Burnside that the mine should be detonated as quickly as possible before the tunnel's dampness might disable the fragile fuse.

Carrying powder to the mine

3

"WE LOOKS LIKE MEN ER WAR"

The successful completion of the mine caught Meade somewhat by surprise. Never believing that Pleasants could complete the project, the general had paid little attention to Burnside's overall attack plan. On the night of July 29, as he finally listened to the enthusiastic Burnside describe the proposal in excruciating detail, Meade dourly objected to one of the most basic components of the plan.

Burnside proposed to lead the assault with the two brigades of the United States Colored Troops of General Edward Ferrero's Fourth Division. His rationale was sound to the extent that Ferrero's men were reasonably fresh troops, having been spared the continuous shelling of the front line. As such, he believed they would be more inclined to make the attack with reckless determination than the front-line white divisions which had become conditioned to seek shelter under fire. For weeks, Burnside had directed Ferrero to drill his men in the complex maneuvers of the assault he envisioned. Immediately following the mine's detonation, Ferrero was to lead his men past the resulting crater and, while detachments peeled off to secure the connecting side-trenches, the main body was to take the ridge 500 feet behind the fort. Then other divisions would pass through Ferrero's Division and take Petersburg.

According to the prevailing attitude, black troops were deemed able to perform rear-echelon chores such as guard

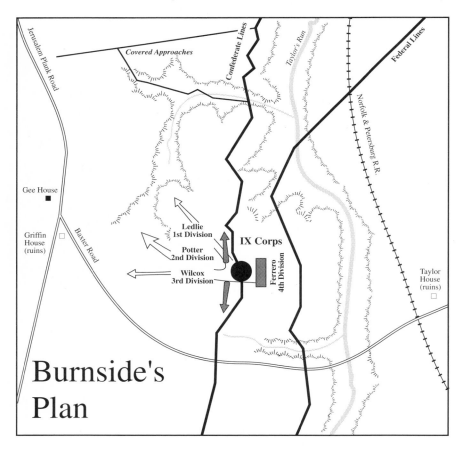

Jerusalem Plank Road

Covered Approaches

Confederate Lines

Taylor's Run

Federal Lines

Norfolk & Petersburg R.R.

Gee House

Griffin House (ruins)

Baxter Road

Ledlie 1st Division

Potter 2nd Division

Wilcox 3rd Division

IX Corps

Ferrero 4th Division

Taylor House (ruins)

Burnside's Plan

duty or manual labor, but incapable of "standing up" under fire. Consequently, ever since its arrival at Petersburg, the Fourth Division had been parceled out to other, white divisions to perform these necessary though menial tasks.

Burnside, however, unlike many of his fellow officers, had faith in his black troops, and they, in turn, were eager to prove themselves in combat. Accordingly, the Fourth Division's two brigade commanders, Colonel Joshua Sigfried and Colonel Henry G. Thomas, had called in their far-flung regiments and

Edward Ferrero: born Spain 1831; raised in New York, he assumed his Italian father's dance instruction school, teaching dancing to West Point cadets; active in the New York militia, he was lieutenant colonel at the outbreak of the Civil War; he

was mustered into the volunteer army as colonel of the 51st New York Infantry; he took part in General Ambrose Burnside's North Carolina Expedition during the winter of 1862-63 and led a brigade at Second Bull Run; promoted to brigadier general of volunteers, he led a brigade at Antietam and Fredericksburg; his commission went unconfirmed and expired in March 1863; he was nonetheless reappointed and confirmed two months later; transferred to the Western Theater, he commanded a brigade in the Vicksburg Campaign; at Knoxville in November 1863, he demonstrated a marked lack of leadership while commanding a division in Burnside's Ninth Corps; returning to Virginia with the Ninth Corps, he received command of a new division composed of black troops, which he led during the Overland Campaign and in the investment of Petersburg; Ferrero's Division was initially selected to lead the assault on the Petersburg Crater, but a change in orders left the division entering the fray after the Confederates had recovered substantially; the division was wrecked while Ferrero remained in a bombproof drinking rum with General James Ledlie; although severely chastised by a court of inquiry, Ferrero remained with his division until the end of the war; as evidence of the impropriety of the Federal rewards system Ferrero was brevetted major general for the Petersburg Campaign; after the war he resumed his career as a dance instructor and managed numerous ballrooms in New York. General Ferrero died in New York City in 1899.

George Gordon Meade: born Spain of U.S. parents 1815; graduated from U.S. Military Academy 1835, nineteenth in his class; 2d lieutenant 3rd Artillery 1835; resigned in 1836 to become a civil engineer; re-entered army in 1842 as 2d lieutenant topographical engineers; brevet lst lieutenant 1846 for gallant conduct during Mexican War; lst lieutenant 1851; captain 1856; brigadier general volunteers 1861; advanced from command of a brigade during the Seven Days (wounded at White Oak Swamp) and Second Bull Run to command of a division at Antietam and Fredericksburg, to command of the Fifth Corps at Chancellorsville; brigadier

general U.S. Army 1863; selected by President Lincoln to replace Joseph Hooker as commander of Army of the Potomac rather than the more qualified John F. Reynolds because Meade's foreign birth disqualified him from the presidency; showed remarkable courage in accepting battle at Gettysburg only two days after assuming army command; major general 1864; received thanks of Congress in 1864 for his contributions to Union victory; from the Wilderness to Appomattox, Meade was in the awkward position of commanding the Army of the Potomac while Grant, the overall commander, traveled with Meade's army; battle strain combined with this difficult command situation helped make Meade so unpopular and quarrelsome that Grant seriously considered replacing him; a staff officer said of Meade: "I don't know any thin old gentleman with a hooked nose and cold blue eye, who, when he is wrathy, exercises less of Christian charity than my well-beloved Chief." Grant pronounced Meade "brave and conscientious, ...[a man who] commanded the respect of all who knew him." After the war, he commanded first the Division of the Atlantic and then Reconstruction Military District No. 3 (comprising Alabama, Georgia, and Florida); bitterly disappointed at not being appointed lieutenant general when Sherman replaced Grant as army commander, Meade returned to command the Division of the Atlantic; died of pneumonia in 1872, never having fully recovered from his White Oak Swamp wound.

reorganized them as a combat unit. For weeks they had drilled their troops in the complicated battle maneuvers required for the assault. A new confidence spread through the division's ranks, and as they gathered around their campfires they had expressed their new esprit in a song that was remembered years later by white troops who had heard it in the camps. The melody and rhythm were familiar, taken from the old spirituals the men knew so well, but the lyrics and feeling were new. "We

James H. Ledlie: born New York 1832; he studied at Union College at Schenectady, New York, and became a civil engineer, engaged mostly in railroad construction; following the outbreak of the Civil War, Ledlie joined the 19th New York Infantry as a major and gained promotion to lieutenant colonel in September 1861; the 19th's designation was changed to the 3d New York Light Artillery in December, with Ledlie becoming its colonel shortly thereafter; serving at various posts, mostly along the North Carolina coast, he commanded the artillery brigade of the Eighteenth Corps; promoted to brigadier general of volunteers in December 1862; his appointment expired without confirmation the following March; reappointed and confirmed in October 1863, he received a brigade command in General Ambrose Burnside's Ninth Corps, joining the Army of the Potomac at Spotsylvania Courthouse in May 1864; in June he was given command of the First Division, Ninth Corps; his division was selected to lead the assault following the mine explosion in the Petersburg trenches in July 1864; after poor preparation, the division attacked, only to be mauled by the recovering Confederates; for his part, Ledlie remained hidden in a bombproof, drinking rum with General Edward Ferrero and leaving the direction of the division to his subordinates; Ledlie was heavily criticized by a court of inquiry and widely accused of cowardice and drunkenness by his fellow officers; he went on sick leave a week after the Battle of the Crater and, seeing no further duty, resigned in January 1865; following the war he resumed his career as a railroad engineer. General Ledlie died at Staten Island in 1882. He is generally considered one of the war's most incompetent commanders.

looks like men a marchin' on, we looks like men er war."

Now, with the projected assault only hours away, Meade, with Grant's approval, informed Burnside that his black division would not be the first unit in the assault, but the last. Meade's reasoning was the complete antithesis to that of the Ninth Corps commander. In later testimony before the court of inquiry, Meade explained that the Fourth Division was "a new division, and had never been under fire—had never been tried—and as this was an operation which I knew beforehand was one requiring the best troops, I thought it impolitic to trust it...." Burnside, nearly frantic with frustration, pled with his superior, but Meade was firm. His final argument was more political than military. As Grant later recounted, "General Meade said that if we put the colored troops in front (we had only one division) and it should prove a failure, it would then be said, and very properly, that we were shoving these people

Orlando Bolivar Willcox: born Michigan 1823; graduated U.S. Military Academy 1847, eighth in a class of thirty-eight; 2d lieutenant 4th artillery 1847; served briefly in Mexico City and Cuernavaca at the end of the Mexican War and then in New Mexico, Massachusetts, and Florida; promoted to 1st lieutenant 1850; participated in actions against the Seminole Indians in 1856 and 1857; resigned from the army 1857 to practice law in Detroit; in May 1861 appointed colonel 1st Michigan Volunteer Infantry; "voluntarily led repeated charges" until wounded and captured while commanding a brigade in Heintzelman's Division at First Bull Run; remained a prisoner for more than a year; upon his release in 1862 appointed brigadier general of volunteers to rank from the date of his capture and assigned command of a division in Burnside's Ninth Corps; led his division, and sometimes the Ninth Corps, at Antietam, Fredericksburg, Knoxville, and during Grant's Virginia campaign in 1864; after Burnside left the Amry of the Potomac after the Crater debacle, Willcox seemed his logical successor, but corps command went instead to John G. Parke. Willcox continued to command his division

ahead to get killed because we did not care anything about them. But that could not be said if we put white troops in front." Meade's final orders were emphatic; there would be no more discussion on the subject.

With the assault only fifteen hours away, Burnside's task was overwhelming. He was faced with rewriting orders to direct four divisions spread over miles of trenches to deploy on a moonless, sweltering night, through unfamiliar territory, and to be prepared to carry out a major assault in the morning. Shortly after noon on July 29, Burnside held his final meeting with the commanders of his three white divisions. Generals Robert Potter and Orlando Bolivar Willcox of the Second and Third divisions were trusted, battle-tried veterans. General James Ledlie, commander of the First Division, somewhat prophetically, arrived late. It was Burnside's duty to choose one of these men to lead the assault.

until the war ended. Brevetted in 1864 major general volunteers for distinguished service, Willcox continued to receive honors: in 1867 brevet brigadier general U.S. Army for gallant service in the Battle of Spottsylvania and major general U.S. Army for gallant service in the capture of Petersburg; in 1895 the Congressional Medal of Honor for "most distinguished gallantry" at Bull Run thirty-four years earlier. After the war Willcox returned to Detroit to practice law, but upon enlargement of the regular army he became colonel of the 29th Infantry in 1866; transferred to the 12th Infantry in 1869, and served at San Francisco almost continuously until 1878, when he took command of the Department of Arizona during the height of warfare with the Apaches and remained until 1882; the town of Willcox, Arizona, was named for him; promoted to brigadier general in 1886, he retired from the army the following year; in 1889 he became governor of the Soldiers' Home in Washington; moved to Coburg, Ontario, in 1905, where he died in 1907. He was buried in Arlington National Cemetery. Twice married; first, in 1852, to Marie Louise Farnsworth of Detroit; second, to Julia Elizabeth (McReynolds) Wyeth, widow of Charles J. Wyeth of Detroit, Willcox had six children, five by his first marriage and one by the second. He authored an artillery manual and two novels dealing with army life and with Detroit, both published under the pen name of "Walter March"--Shoepac Recollections: A Way-side Glimpse of American Life (1856) and Faca, an Army Memoir (1857).

Utterly beaten and drained by his conference with Meade, Burnside could not bring himself to make a decision. As he faced the three men in his tent, none appeared to be a better choice than the others. His next move was to prove damaging to him in the court of inquiry. He put three slips of paper into his hat and asked his division commanders to draw lots. Ledlie, by most accounts a drunkard and a coward, drew the odd lot.

Called by Grant "the worst commander in his corps," James Ledlie had somehow managed to attain the rank of brigadier general during the last three years of war. His staff, constantly scrambling to cover their boss's ineptitude, had developed an intense dislike for the man; some loathed him. Burnside, never a great judge of character, was completely unaware of his alcoholic general's shortcomings. His oversight was to cost him both a battle and a career.

4

"A SPECTACLE OF APPALLING GRANDEUR"

The night of July 30 was a bedlam of activity. As the leading Union divisions moved up to the staging areas, troops moving in to reman their lines became lost in the pitch-black maze of trenches and covered ways. Commanders became separated from their units and conflicting orders added to the chaos. Miraculously, Ledlie's men arrived in position on schedule and waited nervously in the hot, airless covered ways leading to the front. As 3:30 A.M., the detonation time, approached, officers checked and rechecked their pocket watches. As an officer of the 48th Pennsylvania recalled, "Who can forget that morning, or the stillness of that hour! The covered ways were crowded with troops ready to spring into action as soon as the mine was sprung." As the tension mounted, 3:30 came and passed. Meade, in a frenzy of anticipation, repeatedly wired

Burnside for news. Burnside, in turn, dispatched an aide to Pleasants down at the mine entrance. The entire project was in jeopardy. The plan called for a night assault and dawn was little more than an hour away. As the Pennsylvania officer remembered, "Pleasants became like a maniac—he knew where the defect was—those spliced fuses would defeat his great project!"

Finally, at 4:15 A.M., Pleasants allowed Sergeant Henry Reese into the shaft to check the fuses. Nervously scurrying down the silent tunnel, the veteran miner was only too aware that the defective fuse could merely be smoldering and could

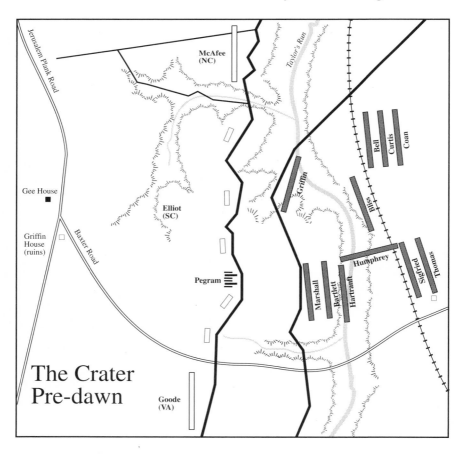

The Crater
Pre-dawn

burst into flame at any moment. Deep within the earth, he would be buried alive if the charge ignited. At last, over halfway to the four tons of powder, Sergeant Reese discovered that the fuse had indeed gone out at one of the splices. Not having a knife to cut through the fuse's protective wrapping to reach its flammable core, he desperately turned and made his way towards the entrance to find one. Halfway out, he encountered Lieutenant Jacob Doughty, sent by Pleasants to check on him. Luckily Doughty had a pocketknife and the two men cut away the damp section of fuse and relit the remaining forty feet. As the fuse sputtered behind them, the two men frantically tumbled into the fresh air.

Explosion of the mine

At 4:44 on the morning of July 30, the mine exploded. A captain in the Union trenches would later remember:

> A slight tremor of the earth for a second, then the rocking as of an earthquake, and, with a tremendous blast which rent the sleeping hills beyond, a vast column of earth and smoke shoots upward to a great height, its dark sides flashing out sparks of fire, hangs poised for a moment in mid-air, and then, hurtling down with a roaring sound, showers of stones, broken timbers and blackened human limbs, subsides — the gloomy pall of darkening smoke flashing to an angry crimson as it floats away to meet the morning sun.

One of Ledlie's men described the scene before him as a "spectacle...of appalling grandeur."

It was an experience for which none of the men could have prepared. As 164 Union cannon and mortars simultaneously opened fire on the Confederate lines, "the sounds were perfectly deafening." According to a New Yorker, "the men became frantic with excitement." Many of Ledlie's men panicked and bolted for the rear, only to be pushed back by their officers. Others merely gaped, open-mouthed, as the sky began to rain debris. It took as many as fifteen crucial minutes for them to recover their senses and begin the attack.

As Ledlie's men jostled through the narrow covered ways, they found their paths choked by men ahead. Those who at last made it to the forward trench found that Burnside had failed to order the parapets lowered for their crossing. Engineers had constructed two narrow sandbag stairways, but these proved hopelessly inadequate to provide passage for the thousands of troops. A major of a New York regiment described the desperation of his men: "Our own works, which were very high at this point, had not been prepared for scaling....ladders were improvised by the men placing their bayonets between the logs in the works and holding the other end....thus forming steps over which men climbed." Once beyond their trenches and in no-man's-land, the troops were further slowed by their own abatis and other infantry obstacles which Burnside had also forgotten to order removed. As his division jostled past, Ledlie paused to watch as Colonel Elisha G. Marshall and the one-legged General William F. Bartlett led their brigades into the smoke. Ledlie then ducked out of sight.

Elisha G. Marshall: born New York 1829; graduated from the U.S. Military Academy in 1850, twenty-fifth in his class of forty-four that included future Union Generals G.K. Warren and Eugene Carr; brevetted 2d lieutenant of infantry; promoted to 2d lieutenant in May 1851 and 1st lieutenant in March 1855, he served on the frontier and in the Utah Expedition of 1858; promoted to captain in May 1861; following the outbreak of the Civil War he worked with New York volunteers, transferring to the volunteer organization himself as colonel of the 13th New York Infantry in April 1862; he led the regiment in the Peninsular Campaign, the Seven Days' Battles, Second Bull Run, and Antietam; brevetted major in the regular army; severely wounded at Fredericksburg in December 1862, he was brevetted lieutenant colonel in the regular army; disabled until May 1863, he mustered out of the 13th New York; commissioned colonel of the 14th New York Heavy Artillery (serving as infantry) in January 1864; he led the regiment in the Wilderness, at Spotsylvania Courthouse, and during the Overland Campaign; wounded at Petersburg in June 1864, he was back with his regiment for the July assault on the Crater, where he was captured; imprisoned at Columbus, Georgia, until the end of the war, he was brevetted colonel in the regular army for Petersburg and brigadier general in both regular and volunteer organizations for war service; returning to duty, he commanded an occupation brigade  in Virginia until July 1865 and was mustered out of the volunteer army in August; continuing in the regular army as major in the 5th Infantry, he was retired with the rank of colonel due to disability caused by his war wounds in 1867. Colonel Marshall died at Canadaigua, New York, in 1883.

The first men who finally reached the site of the exploded fort stared awestruck at the hellish scene before them. One of them remembered, "In the pit, powder smoke issued from the crevices; guns were seen half buried; the heads or limbs of half-buried men wriggled in the loose earth." The chasm left by the mine was sixty feet across, nearly two hundred feet wide, and from ten to thirty feet in depth. Forgetting their instructions, many men slid down the steep sandy walls of the Crater and began digging half-buried Confederates out of the wreck-

William F. Bartlett: born Massachusetts 1840; a student at Harvard at the outbreak of the Civil War, he enlisted as a private in the 4th Massachusetts Battalion; he returned to school briefly, but in August 1861 joined the 20th Massachusetts as a captain; although a wound received at Yorktown in the spring of 1862 forced the amputation of a leg, he managed to graduate with his Harvard class of 1862 in June; he mustered out in November to become colonel of the 49th

Massachusetts; joining the command of General N.P. Banks in Louisiana, Bartlett was twice wounded in the attack on Port Hudson; again mustered out, he returned to Massachusetts to raise a regiment for service in the Army of the Potomac; leading his new regiment, the 57th Massachusetts, he was wounded again in the Battle of the Wilderness in May 1864; promoted to brigadier general of volunteers, he took command of a brigade in General Ambrose Burnside's Ninth Corps; during the Battle of the Crater on 30 July 1864, Bartlett received his fifth wound, and with his bullet-riddled artificial leg torn away he was finally compelled to surrender; held at Libby Prison for two months before being exchanged, he rejoined the Army of the Potomac as commander of the First Division, Ninth Corps following the close of hostilities; brevetted major general U.S. Volunteers, he was mustered out for the final time in July 1866; following the war he worked at the Tredegar Iron Works in Richmond. General Bartlett died at Pittsfield, Massachusetts, in 1876, at the age of thirty-six. Despite his many wounds and diminished mobility, he continued to display remarkable courage in personally

age of the fort. In all, some 278 South Carolinians had been killed or wounded by the blast. Those who had miraculously survived were quickly sent to the rear as prisoners.

Jolted awake by the explosion and accompanying barrage, most of the Confederates around Elliott's Salient panicked and ran for their lives. Their headlong flight created a four-hundred-foot gap in the already undermanned Rebel defenses leading over the Jerusalem Plank Road and directly into Petersburg. A few of the more intrepid Federals made their way into the trench directly behind the Crater but there they stopped. Leaderless, without any concept of a battle plan, the First Division was nothing more than a rabble of confused, frightened men, helpless to exploit the opportunity that Pleasants' men had labored so long to provide.

As his troops milled about aimlessly in the distant Confederate works, General Ledlie was nowhere to be found. Before the last of his division had cleared the Union trenches, the general had begged his way into Surgeon O.P. Chubb's improvised operating room in a converted bombproof. There, sick with fright, he cajoled the physician out of a bottle of medicinal rum under the unlikely pretext of having been painfully bruised by a spent bullet. For good measure he also added that he was feeling quite ill. While the skeptical doctor prepared his field dressings, the division commander huddled in the corner with his bottle.

As the Federal advance broke down, the Confederates began to rally. Having first panicked, the survivors of Elliott's Salient soon clambered back into the works on either side of the Crater and began picking targets among the disorganized mob. At first only a smattering of rifle shots, the Confederate fire soon picked up in intensity. As more Rebels filled the rifle pits and traverses around the Crater, they were able to bring the Federals under a withering crossfire from three directions. While the Rebel infantry kept Ledlie's men pinned down in and around the Crater, two batteries of twelve-pounder Napoleons opened up with shrapnel and canister. The four-gun Wright's Battery, about 500 yards to the north, and one gun of Davidson's Battery, across Baxter Road and 400 yards south, were, according to one of the gunners, "sweeping the open field like a tornado." Within minutes the Rebel smoothbores had carpeted the ground between the opposing trenches with hundreds of dead and wounded Federals.

Into this firestorm General Simon G. Griffin led the Second Brigade of Potter's Second Division. Initially maintaining good order, the Second Division fought its way slightly beyond and to the right of Ledlie's men sheltering in the Crater. Their

Simon G. Griffin: born New Hampshire 1824; he taught school, studied law, and served in the state legislature; in 1860 he was admitted to the bar; following the outbreak of the Civil War, Griffin was appointed a captain in the 2d New Hampshire Infantry; beginning a war-long association with General Ambrose Burnside, Griffin fought in that general's brigade at First Bull Run; he resigned in October 1861 to become lieutenant colonel of the 6th New Hampshire, with which he participated in Burnside's North Carolina Expedition in the winter of 1861-62; promoted to colonel, he led the regiment at Second Bull Run, Antietam, and Fredericksburg; transferred to the Western Theater with the Ninth Corps, he served during the Vicksburg Campaign of 1863; Griffin spent several months in New Hampshire recruiting and organizing new regiments; he returned to the Eastern Theater with the Ninth Corps, joining the Army of the Potomac during General U.S. Grant's Overland Campaign of 1864; promoted to brigadier general of volunteers that May, he commanded a brigade, and occasionally the Second Division, during the investment of Petersburg; brevetted major general for his services there, he was mustered out of the volunteer army in August 1865; following the war he returned to New Hampshire, where he engaged in manufacturing and served two terms in the state legislature; he also twice ran unsuccessfully for Congress and spent several years in Texas involved in railroad and land speculation. General Griffin died at Keene, New Hampshire, in 1902.

advance was slowed as elements of Bartlett's Brigade became intermixed with their ranks and a desperate hail of rifle fire from a few outnumbered survivors of the 17th South Carolina on the ridge behind the Crater thinned their ranks. Still, Potter's men pressed on, their superior numbers and return fire prompting some of the Rebels to run for their lives.

Just as the South Carolinians began to break, the 49th North Carolina under Lieutenant Colonel John Flemming arrived at the double-quick. Heartened by the reinforcements, the South Carolinians returned to their positions behind the Salient and joined the Tarheels in a withering fire on the still advancing Federals. With their officers frantically shouting encouragement, the men loaded and reloaded, firing furiously. Colonel Flemming was killed, shot through the head, but as a battery of mortars on the ridge joined the crossfire from Captain Samuel T. Wright's Battery, the Federal attack wavered. Unsupported by Ledlie and losing heavy casualties, the lead Federal troops, men of the 31st Maine under Colonel Daniel White, had gained only about 200 yards. Now, the combined Rebel fire forced the stubborn 31st back toward the Crater.

John A. Flemming was a farmer before the war. He joined the 49th North Carolina Infantry in February 1862 as a captain and by July 1864 he was commanding the regiment. While leading his troops in the Battle of the Crater, Colonel Flemming was shot through the head and instantly killed.

As more Federal troops crowded into the narrow front, communications began to fall apart. In the Crater, Ledlie's subordinate officers tried desperately to untangle the increasingly vague orders from their distant commander. Burnside further added to the confusion by failing to keep Meade informed of his whereabouts. The resulting flurry of misdirected telegraph messages fueled the animosity between the two generals.

Finally, despite the chaotic situation on his front, Burnside acquiesced to Meade's prodding and issued orders for Ferrero to advance his black division. As the troops of Ferrero's Fourth Division anxiously waited in the stifling covered ways, Burnside's aide searched for their commander, finding him at last, not with his men, but in the surgeon's bombproof with Ledlie. The general issued the necessary orders to advance and then returned to his drinking companion. His men were on their own.

Eager to prove themselves, the men of the Fourth Division attacked. Led by Lieutenant Colonel Joshua K. Sigfried's First Brigade, the United States Colored Troops stormed across the canister-swept no-man's-land toward the Confederate works. Preserving good order but severely punished by the intense Rebel fire, Sigfried's brigade veered slightly and tumbled into the Crater. They maintained their momentum, however, rushed through the confused mob at the bottom of the pit, and emerged on the other side, continuing their attack. Following regiments of the Fourth Division became entangled in the mass of disorganized white troops and stopped. Despite the confusion and fierce Confederate resistance, elements of Ferrero's men pushed several hundred yards beyond their white comrades, capturing some 100 Rebel prisoners and a Confederate flag, and recapturing a Union flag lost by one of the white divisions.

5
"INTO THE MOUTH OF HELL"

While Burnside and Meade squabbled over the telegraph wires, the Confederate leadership was remarkably effective. Upon hearing of the crisis at his headquarters near the Appomattox, General Robert E. Lee immediately dispatched orders to the wiry, 125-pound General William Mahone to send two of his brigades to General Bushrod Johnson as reinforcements. Mahone already knew the situation was serious. Only about a mile above Elliott's Salient when the explosion occurred, Mahone had quickly ridden to investigate. Out of the din of the Union barrage emerged "a soldier, who, from thereabouts, hatless, shoeless, passed me, still going and only time to say `Hell has busted.'" When informed of Lee's orders, the combative little general responded, "I can't send my brigades to General Johnson, I will go with them myself." Ordering Colonel David Weisiger's Virginia and Lieutenant Colonel Mathew Hall's Georgia brigades ahead, Mahone made a quick detour to Johnson's headquarters for news.

Arriving at Johnson's headquarters, Mahone was astounded to find the general fussily attending to a late breakfast. Preoccupied with his morning meal, the hungry Johnson declined Mahone's request to accompany him to the front. Instead, Johnson ordered a lieutenant on his staff to lead Mahone across the Jerusalem Plank Road and through a covered way to the ridge behind the Crater. Just two hundred yards away, the startled general faced eleven Union regimental flags crammed into a mere hundred yards of the captured Rebel works. Although the thousands of Union troops seemed

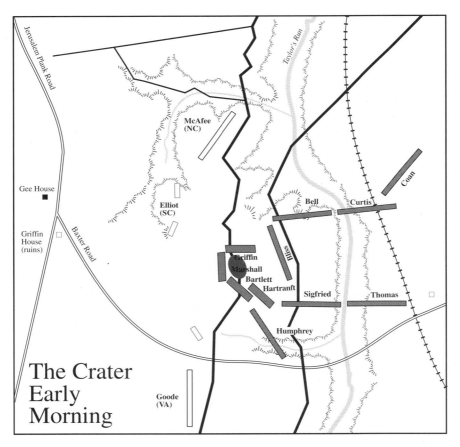

The Crater
Early
Morning

"greatly disordered," Mahone quickly sent back to his division for another brigade, Colonel John Caldwell Calhoun Sanders's Alabamians.

In the teeming mass of Federals before the Confederate general, Colonel Henry Thomas gamely tried to rally his stalled Second Brigade of Ferrero's Division. With most of its white officers dead or wounded, the Second Brigade was pinned

William Mahone: born Virginia 1826; a 1847 graduate of the Virginia Military Institute, he taught at Rapahannock Military Institute and studied engineering; entering the railroad industry in Virginia, he was superintendent of the Norfolk and Petersburg line at the time of Virginia's secession; appointed quartermaster general of Virginia, he soon entered Confederate service as colonel of the 6th Virginia Infantry; after taking part in the capture of the Norfolk Navy Yard he was promoted to brigadier general; he commanded the Norfolk District until it was evacuated in the spring of 1862; joining what would become the Army of Northern Virginia, he led a brigade in the Seven Days' Battles and at Second Manassas, where he was wounded; rejoining his brigade in December 1862, he fought continuously with the Army of Northern Virginia for the balance of the war, seeing action in every major battle from Fredericksburg to Appomattox; Mahone assumed direction of General R.H. Anderson's Division when that officer took direction of the First Corps following the wounding of General James Longstreet in May 1864; during the intense fighting that followed the Petersburg mine explosion Mahone's Division spearheaded the counterattack that restored the Confederate line;

for his conduct at the Crater he received an on-the-field promotion to major general from General Robert E. Lee; given permanent direction of the division, Mahone led it with distinction for the remainder of the conflict, becoming one of Lee's most reliable commanders; after the war he returned to railroading; he angered many former Confederates with his involvement in Republican politics; after a failed gubernatorial bid he was elected to the U.S. Senate in 1880. "Little Billy" Mahone died at Washington, D.C., in 1895. Mahone was a Civil War anomaly. After a lackluster career as a brigade commander, he excelled when given the higher responsibility of directing a division.

down in and around the western edge of the Crater. Suddenly, in a grand gesture to inspire the frightened troops, Lieutenant Christopher Pennell vaulted out of the works and with his regimental guidon in one hand and his sword in the other, shouted for his troops to follow. The Confederate response was immediate and deadly. Suddenly the target of dozens of South Carolinians, Pennell lurched as the first bullet struck him, and then the air around him filled with mini balls, "whirling him round and round several times," as Thomas remembered. As the young lieutenant spun about, his red sash whipping about

Bushrod R. Johnson: born Ohio 1817; graduated from the U.S. Military Academy in 1840, twenty-third in his class of forty-two that included W.T. Sherman, G.H. Thomas, and R.S. Ewell; commissioned 2d lieutenant and posted to the 3d Infantry, he served on the frontier, in the Seminole War, and in Mexico; promoted to 1st lieutenant in February 1844; he resigned his commission in 1847 to become

an educator; an instructor and administrator at the Western Military Institute in Kentucky and the Military College of the University of Nashville, Johnson was also active in both the Kentucky and Tennessee militias; he entered Confederate service as a colonel of engineers in June 1861 and was appointed brigadier general the following January; forced to surrender with the garrison at Fort Donelson in February 1862, he managed to escape through Union lines; wounded while leading a brigade at Shiloh, he recovered to lead his brigade in General Braxton Bragg's invasion of Kentucky and at Murfreesboro; commanded a provisional division at Chickamauga and directed General Simon B. Buckner's Division at Knoxville; transferred to the Eastern Theater, he led a brigade in the early defense of Petersburg; promoted to major general, he commanded a division in the Petersburg trenches and took part in restoring the Confederate line during the Battle of the Crater in July 1864; relieved of duty after his division was destroyed at Saylor's Creek in April 1865, he was without a command when he surrendered at Appomattox; after the war he became chancellor of the University of Nashville. General Johnson died at his farm near Brighton, Illinois, in 1880.

his waist, he lost his grip of the flag and his sword, and, as the firing subsided, pitched headfirst to the Virginia clay. According to another officer, a number of the Union troops "were shot because, spellbound, they forgot their own shelter in watching this superb boy, who was the only child of an old Massachusetts clergyman...." Horror-stricken, Pennell's men clung even tighter to the sparse shelter around the Crater.

In the meantime, General Ferrero somewhat unsteadily left the surgeon's bombproof to try to get some idea of his division's whereabouts. Still safely out of range of the Confederate rifle fire, the general could make out few details of his Fourth

David A. Weisiger: born Virginia 1818; a merchant, he served with Virginia volunteers in the War with Mexico; active in the state militia, he was present at the hanging of John Brown and during the evacuation of the Norfolk Navy Yard; commissioned colonel of the 12th Virginia Infantry; he served on the Peninsula and during the Seven Days' Battles; at Second Manassas he succeeded the wounded General William Mahone as brigade commander only to be severely wounded himself; disabled for more than a year, Weisiger did not rejoin the Army of Northern Virginia until July 1863; he led his regiment in the Battle of the Wilderness; when Mahone assumed command of the division, Weisiger took direction of Mahone's Brigade with the temporary rank of brigadier general; he led the brigade at Spotsylvania and throughout the Overland Campaign; during the Battle of the Crater in July 1864, he was again wounded while conspicuously leading his brigade; promoted, on the field, to the permanent rank of brigadier general by General Robert E. Lee, he was also given permanent command of the brigade, which he led with

distinction for the remainder of the war; he surrendered with the Army of Northern Virginia at Appomattox Courthouse in April 1865; after the war he was a banker in Petersburg and later engaged in business in Richmond. In the aftermath of the Battle of the Crater Weisiger openly feuded with Mahone over who was the rightful "Hero of the Crater." He died at Richmond in 1899 without receiving what he believed to be his just recognition.

Division's actions, obscured as they were by distance, battle smoke and, possibly, his own self-induced haze. After hurriedly dispatching some rather general orders to Colonel Thomas concerning capturing Cemetery Hill and the Gee House, now Confederate headquarters, Ferrero again slipped back out of sight. The general showed no inkling that he understood the grave situation of his inexperienced black troops as they faced Mahone's quickly arriving veterans.

Shortly before nine o'clock, Mahone, spotting Ferrero's men preparing for another advance, hurriedly urged his men into action. Pointing toward the commander of his lead brigade of

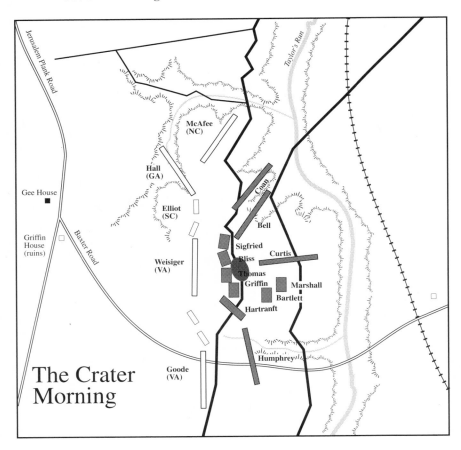

The Crater
Morning

Virginians, he frantically shouted, "Tell Weisiger to forward."
Filling the morning air with the shrill Rebel Yell, the
Virginians, soon joined by a few North and South Carolinians,
swept down the slope with fixed bayonets. Survivors of the
earlier fighting had inflamed Weisiger's men with the informa-
tion that the black troops before them had stormed the
Confederate works with the battle cries, "No quarter to the
Rebels" and "Remember Fort Pillow."

The Fort Pillow battle cry referred to the ill-fated fort in
Tennessee in which General Nathan Bedford Forrest's
Confederates allegedly massacred a number of black soldiers.
The recent incident was widely covered by the northern press
and contributed to the ferocity of the fighting between black
troops seeking vengeance and their Confederate foes. A veteran of the action recalled that Mahone's men truly felt that "to
be captured by the negro troops meant death not only to our-
selves but, it appeared, to the helpless women and children in
Petersburg."

The fierce Confederate counterattack threw Ferrero's
troops into a panic. Their rifles emptied after the first volley,
Mahone's men leapt into the first trench with their bayonets,
killing everyone in their path. A quarter century later, the bar-
barity of two of his comrades' treatment of a cornered black
sergeant still haunted a veteran of the fight as he recalled "one
of them striking the poor wretch with a steel ramrod." The soldier continued to beat the helpless man as the other repeatedly emptied his rifle into him and finally, "placing the muzzle
close against the stomach of the poor negro, fired, at which
the latter fell limp and lifeless...." As the maddened Rebels
swept the trench, Ferrero's men, most in combat for the first
time, threw away their rifles and scrambled over the labyrinth
of trenches toward the Crater.

All along the captured works, panic turned to rout as
Ferrero's troops threw down their rifles and crashed back into
their huddled white comrades. The terror-stricken men were

crowded so thickly into the narrow traverses that many could not move their arms to fight back or even to beg for mercy. Others, in their panic, scrambled over the heads of the men trapped in the traverses to reach the rear. The outnumbered Confederate troops ranged freely about the trenches firing point-blank into the Federals, occasionally sending a white soldier to the rear as a prisoner.

As the Federals plunged back into the relative safety of the Crater, they left their former trenches filled with the dead and dying. A North Carolinian remembered, "the Yankee dead lay in heaps between the works, the wounded trying to crawl out from under the dead." The Confederates also had suffered heavy casualties in their fearless charge through the hail of canister and rifle fire. Stumbling among the blue and gray jacketed corpses, Mahone's men were at times up to their ankles in the dead men's blood. By now, however, the momentum was on the Confederates' side as reinforcements converged on the Crater.

By ten o'clock, with most of the Union troops jammed into the Crater, Mahone closed in for the kill. Confederate Colonel John Haskell's two small Coehorn mortars were by then so close to the Crater that his men were using only one-and-a-quarter-ounce powder charges to lob their heavy shells into the pit. As the projectiles slowly arced over the rim, he could hear the trapped men's screams as, wide-eyed, they watched the hissing shells descend. The resulting explosions sent men and human body parts flying, and more screams followed as the wounded pled for help. Brevet Major Charles H. Houghton of the 14th New York Heavy Artillery recalled: "No air was stirring within the crater. It was a sickening sight: men were dead and dying all around us; blood was streaming down the sides of the crater to the bottom, where it gathered in pools for a time before being absorbed by the hard red clay."

Many of the Ninth Corps survivors in the Crater had been under constant fire for nearly five hours. A few of Potter's men prepared for a last stand as they scrambled into position along the Crater's edge. Isolated within a mere two-acre area, thousands of men held on as their leaders argued far to the rear. As he watched the far Union flags bunching back into the Crater, General Meade became convinced the attack had failed. Burnside, equally convinced that his pet project could be saved, argued vainly with his commander, but to no avail.

Back in the Crater, General Bartlett was alive but his cork leg was shattered and useless. Desperately, General John F. Hartranft of Willcox's Third Division tried to rally the men while artillerymen of the 14th New York directed a makeshift battery of two captured Napoleons. Furiously loading and reloading their two guns with canister, the New Yorkers fought desperately to keep the Rebels at bay.

Carefully aiming from his exposed perch on the Crater's rim, Sergeant James Lathe dropped his fifth Confederate of the day. As he searched for a sixth victim, a Confederate's bullet tore his hand in half, tumbling him shrieking down the steep inner slope. His companions kept up their desperate defense even as Confederate artillerymen wrestled their field guns into positions to fire directly into gaps in the Crater's walls. The fire was so devastating that "General Bartlett ordered the colored troops to build a breastworks across it. They commenced the work by throwing up lumps of clay, but it was slow work; some one called out, 'Put in the dead men,'...a large number of dead, white and black, Union and rebel, were piled into the trench.... Cartridges were running low, and we searched the boxes of all the dead and wounded."

To make matters worse, after six hours of continuous fighting in the July heat, the men in the Crater had long since emptied their canteens. Although a few brave men crossed and recrossed the fire-swept no-man's-land to fetch water, only a fraction of the troops could get even a swallow from the battered canteens. Most staggered about panting in the dense heat. The wounded begged piteously for even a drop of water.

As his men struggled for their lives, Burnside could no longer ignore orders from both Meade and Grant. Convinced that there was no longer any hope of success, Meade persuaded Grant to endorse orders to retreat. Around noon, Burnside at last dispatched a courier to the survivors in the Crater with the new orders. General Bartlett, under heavy fire, and his troops "a rabble" could only order his men to hold out until nightfall. Only then did he feel that his command could make a run for safety under cover of darkness. Some men, in their desperation, tried to dig a trench back to their lines using bayonets and their bare hands.

As the Federal commanders wavered and bickered, Mahone brought up the last of his fresh troops. He knew that by stripping the men from his right, he was dangerously vulnerable from that direction; but his fighting blood was up and he was determined to retake the captured fort. Instructing his officers to lead their men as quietly as possible to the edge of the pit to avoid the raking artillery fire, Mahone reminded the men that the black troops they faced were taking no prisoners. In parting, the general told the men that General Lee was watching them from his temporary headquarters in the Gee house on the crest of the ridge above them.

Determined to please their beloved commander, the soldiers made for the pit. As their lines swept past, the remnants of other Rebel units in their path fell alongside and together they scrambled up the outer banks of the Crater. Despite a few scattered shots from the most determined Federals, the Rebels took the rim where General Bartlett was dismayed to see a Rebel flag only feet away.

With the Rebels so close, the situation in the Crater was nothing short of pandemonium. Maddened with the fear of being captured with black troops, many of the white Federals turned on Ferrero's men, shooting and bayonetting them. As the Union troops fought among themselves, more Confederates gathered around the outside. A Confederate captain remembered "a novel method of fighting," as he called it. "There was quite a number of abandoned muskets with bayonets on them, lying on the ground around the fort. Our men began pitching them over the embankment, bayonets foremost, trying to harpoon the men inside, and both sides threw over cannon balls and fragments of shell and earth...."

As the melee reached an even more chaotic level, men on both sides became astonishingly brutal. A soldier in the 35th North Carolina recorded in his diary, "(Lieutenant Thad) Marks seized a broad hatchet and got in action every time a negro's head appeared above the top of the breastworks, Marks cut it off. Just before the negroes were ordered to retreat, an unusually large black fellow ran up and cried out: 'Let Corporal Dick get up; I'll go over.' Corporal Dick went over, but he went over backward and without any head."

Lieutenant Freeman Bowley remembered the action from the inside of the Crater. "A full line around the crest of the crater were loading and firing as fast as they could, and the men were dropping thick and fast, most of them shot through the head. Every man that was shot rolled down the steep sides to the bottom, and in places they were piled up four and five deep.... The cries of the wounded, pressed down under the dead, were piteous in the extreme."

Captain John C. Featherston of the 9th Alabama remembered his experience as entering "into the mouth of hell." Around one o'clock, "Colonel J.H. King ordered the men near him to put their hats on their bayonets and quickly raise them above the fort, which was done, and as he anticipated, they were riddled with bullets." Finally, with a fierce, Rebel Yell, Mahone's men threw themselves over the rim and into the mob of fear-maddened Federals. The savagery only escalated as men emptied their rifles point-blank into their foes and then resorted to stabbing with their bayonets. Men, eyes wide with rage and terror, grappled with bare hands and knives, clubbing one another with rocks and emptied muskets. Some men tried to surrender but when the Confederates continued to shoot the black troops, many retrieved their arms and continued to fight.

Helplessly, General Bartlett looked on as his command disintegrated. Pleas for mercy were drowned out by the constant roar of canister overhead and the din of combat. Four mortally wounded Chippewa Indian sharpshooters who huddled together chanting their death songs added a surreal quality to the hellish scene. Finally, a Confederate officer screamed in the face of a Federal colonel, "Why in the hell don't you fellows surrender?" The colonel's quick reply, "Why the hell don't you let us?" signaled the end of the fighting. Mahone, who had him-

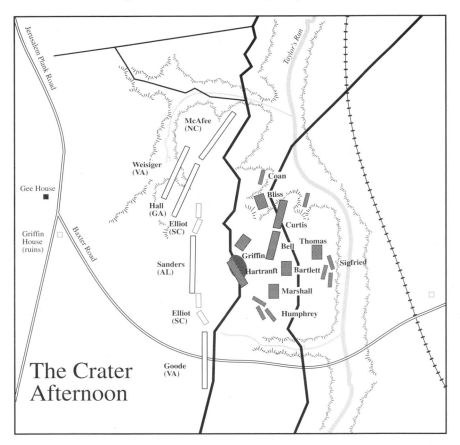

self entered the Crater, guaranteed the Federals' safety and
the exhausted men at last dropped their weapons and car-
tridge boxes.

As his men shuffled under guard to the rear, General
Bartlett, his shattered artificial leg useless, tried to hobble
along with them using two inverted muskets as crutches. A
Confederate captain, impressed with the general's disdain for
such an apparently grave wound, remarked, "that he must
have nerves of steel, as his leg was shot away." Bartlett
"smiled and replied that he had lost his real leg at
Williamsburg two years before, and the leg he had just shattered was a cork leg."

6

"THE SADDEST AFFAIR"

The roughly eight hours of fighting in the Battle of the Crater, as the affair became known, was a disaster for the Federal army. Of the approximate strength of 16,772 men at the Crater, some 3,798 were listed as killed, wounded, or missing. By contrast, of the approximately 9,430 Confederates involved, 1,491 became casualties. The day after the battle, Confederate guards marched the captured Union survivors through the streets of Petersburg to the taunts and jeers of the citizens.

As a reward for his retaking the captured Confederate works, William Mahone was promoted to the rank of major general. General Lee declared that every Confederate soldier involved "made himself a hero." As the Confederate leadership congratulated themselves, their men buried the dead. So many corpses lay in the bottom of the Crater in the summer heat that the Rebels found it easiest merely to cover them over where they lay, incorporating them into the floor of the rapidly rebuilt fort.

In an effort to fix blame for such an embarrassing debacle, Meade called for a court of inquiry. On August 6, less than a week after the battle, the court convened at Second Corps headquarters. Rather ominously for Burnside and the officers of the Ninth Corps, the entire court was composed of Meade's subordinates and friends. Three of the officers detailed to the court, Generals Winfield S. Hancock, Romeyn B. Ayers, and Nelson A. Miles, had all participated in the Crater fighting.

Confederate dead in the trenches of Fort Mahone

Serving as judge advocate, the fourth member, Colonel Edmund Schriver, was also inspector general of Meade's Army of the Potomac.

There must have been little doubt to anyone except, possibly, the naive Burnside, as to the outcome of the investigation. The writing on the wall was most obvious to James Ledlie. In his most decisive maneuver of the war, the First Division commander obtained a twenty-day sick leave and left for home the very day the court convened. Apparently waiting for the dust to settle, he then extended his leave until early December. Immediately after Ledlie returned to duty, Meade, at last fully aware of Ledlie's unique talents, ordered him to return home. He resigned from the army January 23, 1865.

Burnside meanwhile prepared for the trial with all the casualness that characterized his military planning. Accompanied by Generals Potter and Ferrero, he attended the second day of pro-

Dead artilleryman

ceedings as Meade carefully laid the groundwork for the end of Burnside's military career. Angered by what he considered Burnside's insubordination during the battle, and anxious to avoid any personal blame, Meade was both thorough and damning. In page after page of sworn testimony, he outlined the flaws in Burnside's plan and his failures to follow Meade's corrective instructions. Producing documents and witnesses for every indictment, Meade continued as Burnside sat listening helplessly, raising only occasional plaintive objections.

Meade was so adept at assigning guilt for the fiasco that no one raised the issue that he, as Burnside's superior, could have stopped the operation at any time. His testimony instead portrays Burnside and the officers of the Ninth Corps as betraying his good faith and confidence. Meade was skeptical of the plan from the very beginning, but Burnside's enthusiastic insistence swayed him into allowing it to progress despite his reservations.

Once approved, the project assumed a life of its own, doomed to failure, but immune to any attempts to stop it. Although dangerously flawed, Burnside's original conception did have some promise of success. Meade's attempts to correct his oversights, however, only added to the confusion and the animosity between the two men. Still, both Grant and Meade allowed Burnside to continue with the minimal supervision that most officers of his rank would require. Unfortunately, further testimony only served to support their apprehensions in regard to his abilities.

Burnside's testimony in his own defense revealed many of his deficiencies as a commander. In sharp contrast to Meade's direct and lucid statements, he admitted his own remarks were "disjointed" and merely offered a series of unconvincing excuses for his failure. In the process, he betrayed his own tenuous grasp of military realities. Distracted by the novelty of the mine, Burnside failed to comprehend the very crux of the assault plan.

The most crucial element of the attack lay in the speed of exploiting the confusion in the Confederate defenses immediately following the mine detonation. Speed and surprise were essential. As his testimony clearly indicates, Meade immediately grasped the situation and issued clear orders to Burnside for an efficient, rapid assault. His directions called for Burnside to

Cemetery at City Point

clear his front of obstructions to aid supporting artillery fire and the quick passage of his troops. Anticipating the difficulties of passing through the Crater, Meade ordered Burnside to avoid it, attacking on both sides to quickly capture Cemetery Hill. The orders concluded that "promptitude, rapidity of execution, and cordial co-operation, are essential to success...."

Burnside's failure to follow orders was complete. The court placed the responsibility for the disaster squarely on his shoulders. Equally damaging was his indecision resulting in the choice of Ledlie's Division to lead the attack. There was an uncharacteristic degree of logic in his original choice of Ferrero's Division, but once overruled he could not adapt to the

View of the crater after the battle

change. By resorting to the choosing of lots for such an important decision, he only aroused the contempt of his superiors.

Further highlighting Burnside's failings was his apparent trust in Ledlie. Nearly every officer who had served with the man had noted his shortcomings, and yet Burnside, his immediate superior, appeared totally unaware of his incompetence.

His complete blindness to Ledlie's inability to lead troops was painfully obvious in his defense of the drunken general's actions during the battle:

> I do not know of a single order of mine that was not carried out by my division commanders. I do not know of any lack of energy on their part in carrying out my views and the views of the commanding general, except, possibly, in the case of General Ledlie, who was quite sick on that day, and who I thought afterward ought to have gone to the crater the moment his men were in, but I understand that he was very sick and could hardly have walked that far under the oppressive heat.

Few witnesses in Surgeon Chubb's bombproof would have contested Burnside's assessment of Ledlie's inability to walk. However, they might have disagreed as to the cause.

Burnside's testimony only supports the court's opinion that the attack failed in part due to a lack "of a competent common head at the scene of the assault to direct affairs as occurrences should demand." Burnside had merely betrayed his own incompetence by trusting another incompetent.

Of Burnside's division commanders, only one, General Robert B. Potter of the Second Division, accompanied his men in the attack. By most accounts two were drunk, and the fourth, General Orlando B. Willcox of the Third Division, although exhibiting no signs of cowardice, remained within the Federal lines. Potter's testimony provided stark evidence of the confusion among the other divisions directly caused by their lack of leadership. Lieutenant Colonel Henry Pleasants, although excused from duty that day, volunteered for the assault and, according to Potter, blistered his hand in his vigorous attempts to physically shove Ledlie's troops out of the Crater.

On September 9, 1864, after seventeen intermittent days of

deliberations, the court delivered its findings. As commander of the operation, Burnside was held accountable for disobeying Meade's orders and in general, failing to execute a successful attack. Generals Ledlie and Ferrero were each censured for hiding in the bombproof and failing to lead their divisions in the assault. Colonel Zenas R. Bliss, a brigade commander in Potter's Second Division, was also cited for not accompanying his men to the Crater. General Orlando B. Willcox, commander of the Third Division, was censured on the rather vague grounds that he had failed to exercise "more energy...to cause his troops to go forward...."

The Court's final statement was directed at Burnside alone: "The Court express their opinion that explicit orders should have been given assigning one officer to the command of all the troops intended to engage in the assault when the commanding general was not present in person to witness the operations."

The general was not present to hear the court's findings. After testifying, he left for home for what he intended to be a twenty-day leave. During his absence, however, he learned that Grant had replaced him with the Ninth Corps chief of staff, the very capable Major General John G. Parke, and had no intention of reversing the arrangement. Ambrose Burnside's military career was over. Although the Joint Congressional Committee on the Conduct of the War disagreed with the army's internal court of inquiry by placing the majority of the blame on Meade, the damage was done. After a few months of lobbying unsuccessfully for a new assignment, Burnside resigned from the army on April 15, 1865.

In one of the many ironies of the war, Brigadier General Edward Ferrero, former dancing instructor, retained his command and was, amazingly, promoted. In December 1864, despite his poor performance at the Crater, he was breveted major general for "meritorious service in the present campaign before Richmond and Petersburg." It was, perhaps, a fitting epilogue for what Grant declared "the saddest affair I have witnessed in the War."

The war continued for another eight months after the Crater incident. The vicinity of Elliott's Salient never again saw major action and eventually returned to normal siege activi-

View of the crater after the war was over

ties. After the war, William Griffith, the owner of the property, returned to find his house burned and farm devastated by months of continuous fighting. To help make ends meet, Mr. Griffith converted the still impressive Crater into a tourist attraction complete with souvenir relic shop and a saloon. He

was often known to somewhat reluctantly forgo the twenty-five-cent admission fee for Confederate veterans of the battle. In 1936, the Crater was added to the Petersburg National Military Park and is now open to the public.

Note: The Tables of Organization presented in Appendices A and B refer only to units which actually took part in the Battle of the Crater. They are taken from War of the Rebellion: Official Records of the Union and Confederate Armies, Series I, Volume 40, Part 3, Pages 728–729, 733–735, and 737–738. Republished by The National Historical Society, 1972. Additional information comes from The Petersburg Campaign: The Battle of the Crater, "The Horrid Pit," June 26–August 6, 1864 by Michael Arthur Cavanaugh and William Marvel, Pages 121-127.

APPENDIX A

ORGANIZATION OF FEDERAL FORCES
COMMANDER IN CHIEF
LIEUT. GEN. ULYSSES S. GRANT

ARMY OF THE POTOMAC
MAJ. GEN. GEORGE G. MEADE

PROVOST GUARD
BRIG. GEN. MARSENA R. PATRICK

1st Indiana Cavalry, Company K, Capt. Theodore Majtheny

1st Massachusetts Cavalry, Companies C and D, Capt. Charles F. Adams, Jr.

80th New York Infantry (20th Militia), Col. Theodore B. Gates

3d Pennsylvania Cavalry, Companies A, B, and M, Maj. James W. Walsh

68th Pennsylvania Infantry, Col. Andrew H. Tippin

114th Pennsylvania Infantry, Col. Charles H.T. Collis

VOLUNTEER ENGINEER BRIGADE
BRIG. GEN. HENRY W. BENHAM

15th New York Engineers (five companies), Maj. William A. Ketchum

50th New York Engineers, (A detachment of this regiment was stationed in
     Washington, D.C. with its commander, Col. William H. Pettes. The remain
     ing companies served in the field under subordinates).

BATTALION U. S. ENGINEERS
CAPT. GEORGE H. MENDELL

SIGNAL CORPS
CAPT. BENJAMIN F. FISHER

GUARDS AND ORDERLIES
Independent Company Oneida (New York) Cavalry, Capt. Daniel P. Mann

NINTH ARMY CORPS
MAJ. GEN. AMBROSE E. BURNSIDE

PROVOST GUARD
8th U.S. Infantry, Capt. Milton Cogswell

FIRST DIVISION
BRIG. GEN. JAMES H. LEDLIE

First Brigade
BRIG. GEN. WILLIAM FRANCIS BARTLETT
21st Massachusetts, Capt. William H. Clark
29th Massachusetts, Lieut. Col. Joseph H. Barnes
35th Massachusetts, Capt. J. Wilson Ingell
56th Massachusetts, Capt. Charles D. Lamb
57th Massachusetts, Lieut. Albert Doty
59th Massachusetts, Capt. Ezra P. Gould
100th Pennsylvania, Capt. Joseph H. Pentecost

Second Brigade
COL. ELISHA G. MARSHALL
3rd Maryland Battalion, Lieut. Col. Gilbert P. Robinson
14th New York Heavy Artillery, Maj. Charles Chipman
179th New York (seven companies), Capt. Albert A. Terrill
2nd Pennsylvania Provisional Heavy Artillery, Capt. James W. Haig

Acting Engineers
35th Massachusetts, Capt. Clifton Aurelius Blanchard

SECOND DIVISION
BRIG. GEN. ROBERT B. POTTER

First Brigade
COL. ZENAS R. BLISS
36th Massachusetts, Capt. Thaddeus L. Barker
58th Massachusetts, Capt. Charles E. Churchill
2nd New York Mounted Rifles, Col. John Fisk
51st New York, Capt. George W. Whitman
45th Pennslvania, Capt. Theodore Gregg
48th Pennsylvania, Col. Henry Pleasants
4th Rhode Island, Maj. James T.P. Bucklin

Second Brigade
BRIG. GEN. SIMON G. GRIFFIN
31st Maine, Capt. James Dean
32nd Maine, Capt. Joseph B. Hammond
2nd Maryland, Capt. James H. Wilson
6th New Hampshire, Capt. Samuel G. Goodwin
9th New Hampshire, Capt. John B. Cooper
11th New Hampshire, Capt. Arthur C. Locke
17th Vermont, Capt. Lyman E. Knapp

Acting Engineers
7th Rhode Island, Capt. Percy Daniels

THIRD DIVISION
BRIG. GEN. ORLANDO B. WILLCOX

First Brigade
BRIG. GEN. JOHN HARTRANFT
8th Michigan, Maj. Horatio Belcher
27th Michigan (1st & 2nd Companies Michigan Sharpshooters attached),
Capt. Edward S. Leadbeater
109th New York, Capt. Edwin Evans
13th Ohio Cavalry (dismounted battalion), Col. Noah H. Hixon
51st Pennsylvania, Maj. Lane S. Hart
37th Wisconsin, Col. Samuel Harriman
38th Wisconsin (5 Companies), Lieut. Col. Colwert K. Pier

Second Brigade

COL. WILLIAM HUMPHREY

1st Michigan Sharpshooters, Col. Charles V. De Land

2nd Michigan, Capt. Ebenezer C. Tulloch

20th Michigan, Lieut. Col. Byron M. Cutcheon

24th New York Cavalry (Dismounted), Lieut. Col. Walter C. Newberry

46th New York, Capt. Alphons Serviere

60th Ohio (9th and 10th Companies, Ohio Sharpshooters attached),
    Maj. Martin Avery

50th Pennsylvania, Lieut. Col. Edward Overton, Jr.

Acting Engineers

17th Michigan, Col. Constant Luce

FOURTH DIVISION

BRIG. GEN. EDWARD FERRERO

First Brigade

LIEUT. COL. JOSHUA K. SIGFRIED

27th U.S.C.T., Lieut. Col. Charles J. Wright

30th U.S.C.T., Lieut. Col. Hiram A. Oakman

39th U.S.C.T., Col. Ozora P. Stearns

43rd U.S.C.T. (seven companies), Capt. Jesse Wilkinson

Second Brigade

COL. HENRY GODDARD THOMAS

19th U.S.C.T. (28th U.S.C.T. attached), Lieut. Col. Joseph G. Perkins

23rd U.S.C.T., Col. Cleveland J. Campbell

29th U.S.C.T., Maj. T. Jefferson Brown

31st U.S.C.T., Capt. Thomas Wright

Artillery Brigade

LIEUT. COL. J. ALBERT MONROE

Maine Light, 2nd Battery (B), Capt. Albert F. Thomas

Maine Light, 3rd Battery (C), Capt. Ezekiel R. Mayo

Maine Light, 7th Battery (G), Capt. Adelbert B. Twitchell

Massachusetts Light, 11th Battery, Capt. Edward J. Jones

Massachusetts Light, 14th Battery, Capt. Joseph W.B. Wright

New York Light, 19th Battery, Capt. Edward W. Rogers

New York Light, 27th Battery, Capt. John B. Eaton

New York Light, 34th Battery, Capt. Jacob Roemer
Pennsylvania Light, Battery D, Capt. George W. Durell
Vermont Light, 3rd Battery, Capt. Romeo H. Start
Mortar Battery, Capt. Benjamin F. Smiley

FIFTH CORPS ARTILLERY
Col. Charles S. Wainwright
1st New York Light, Battery B, Lieut. Robert E. Rogers
1st New York Light, Battery E, Lieut. James B. Hazelton
1st New York Light, Battery H, Capt. Charles E. Mink
5th United States, Battery D, Lieut. William E. Van Reed

SIXTH CORPS ARTILLERY
Capt. William Hexamer
Maine Light, 4th Battery (D), Lieut. Charles W. White
New York Light, 3rd Battery, Capt. William A. Harn

ARMY OF THE JAMES
Maj. Gen. Benjamin Butler

Siege Artillery
Col. Henry L. Abbot
1st Connecticut Heavy Artillery, Col. Henry L. Abbot
Company A, Capt. Edward A. Gillet
Company B, Capt. Albert F. Booker
Company M, Capt. Franklin A. Pratt

EIGHTEENTH ARMY CORPS
Maj. Gen. Edward O.C. Ord

TENTH ARMY CORPS
(Attached to the Eighteenth Army Corps)

SECOND DIVISION
Brig. Gen. John W. Turner

First Brigade
COL. N. MARTIN CURTIS
3rd New York, Capt. George W. Warren
112th New York, Lieut. Col. John F. Smith
117th New York, Lieut. Col. Rufus Daggett
142nd New York, Lieut. Col. Albert M. Barney

Second Brigade
LIEUT. COL. WILLIAM B. COAN
47th New York, Capt. Charles A. Moore
48th New York, Capt. William H. Dunbar
76th Pennsylvania, Maj. William S. Diller
97th Pennsylvania, Capt. Isaiah Price

Third Brigade
COL. LOUIS BELL
13th Indiana (3 Companies), Lieut. Samuel M. Zent
9th Maine, Capt. Robert J. Gray
4th New Hampshire, Capt. Frank W. Parker
115th New York, Lieut. Col. Nathan J. Johnson
169th New York, Maj. James A. Colvin

APPENDIX B

ORGANIZATION OF CONFEDERATE FORCES

ARMY OF NORTHERN VIRGINIA
GEN. ROBERT E. LEE

THIRD ARMY CORPS
MAJ. GEN. AMBROSE P. HILL

RICHARD H. ANDERSON'S DIVISION
BRIG. GEN. WILLIAM MAHONE

Mahone's (Virginia) Brigade
COL. DAVID WEISIGER
6th Virginia, Col. George Thomas Rogers
12th Virginia, Capt. Richard W. Jones
16th Virginia, Lieut. Col. Richard Owen Whitehead
41st Virginia, Maj. William H. Etheridge
61st Virginia, Lieut. Col. William H. Stewart

Wilcox (Alabama) Brigade
COL. JOHN C.C. SANDERS
8th Alabama, Capt. M.W. Mordecai
9th Alabama, Col. J. Horace King
10th Alabama, Capt. W.L. Brewster
11th Alabama, Lieut. Col. George Edward Tayloe
14th Alabama, Capt. Elias Folk

Wright's (Georgia) Brigade
LIEUT. COL. MATTHEW R. HALL
3rd Georgia, Lieut. Col. Claiborne Snead
22nd Georgia, Col. George H. Jones
48th Georgia, Lieut. Col. Reuben W. Carswell
64th Georgia, Col. John W. Evans

ARTILLERY
ARMY OF NORTHERN VIRGINIA
BRIG. GEN. WILLIAM N. PENDLETON

FIRST CORPS
LIEUT. COL. FRANK HUGER

Haskell's Battalion
MAJ. JOHN C. HASKELL
Branch (North Carolina) Battery, Capt. Henry G. Flanner
Nelson (Virginia) Battery, Capt. James N. Lamkin

13th Battalion Virginia Light Artillery
MAJ. WADE HAMPTON GIBBS
Company A, Otey Battery, Capt. David Norvell Walker
Company B, Ringgold Battery, Capt. Crispin Dickenson
Company C, Davidson's Battery, Lieut. John H. Chamberlayne
Battery of mortars manned by men from Otey and Ringgold Batteries,
    Lieut. Jack Langhorne

THIRD CORPS
COL. REUBEN LINDSAY WALKER

Pegram's Battalion
LIEUT. COL. WILLIAM J. PEGRAM
Crenshaw's (Virginia) Battery, Capt. Thomas Ellett
Letcher (Virginia) Light Artillery, Capt. Thomas A. Brander

DEPARTMENT OF NORTH CAROLINA AND SOUTHERN VIRGINIA
GEN. PIERRE G.T. BEAUREGARD

JOHNSON'S DIVISION
MAJ. GEN. BUSHROD RUST JOHNSON

Ransom's (North Carolina) Brigade
COL. LEE M. MCAFEE
24th North Carolina, Col. William John Clarke
25th North Carolina, Maj. William Simmons Grady
35th North Carolina, Col. James Theodore Johnson
49th North Carolina, Lieut. Col. John A. Flemming
56th North Carolina, Capt. Lawson Harrill

Elliott's (South Carolina) Brigade

Brig. Gen. Stephen Elliott

17th South Carolina, Col. Fitz William McMaster

18th South Carolina, Capt. R.H. Glenn

22nd South Carolina, Col. David G. Fleming

23rd South Carolina, Capt. E.R. White

26th South Carolina, Col. Alexander D. Smith

Wise's (Virginia) Brigade

Col. J. Thomas Goode

26th Virginia, Capt. Napoleon B. Street

34th Virginia, Maj. John R. Bagby

46th Virginia, Capt. George Norris

59th Virginia, Capt. Henry Wood

HOKE'S DIVISION

Maj. Gen. Robert F. Hoke

Clingman's (North Carolina) Brigade

Brig. Gen. Thomas L. Clingman

61st North Carolina, Col. James Dillard Radcliffe

Colquitt's (Georgia) Brigade (temporarily assigned to Johnson's Division)

Brig. Gen. Alfred H. Colquitt

6th Georgia, Col. John T. Lofton

19th Georgia, Col. James H. Neal

23rd Georgia, Col. James H. Huggins

27th Georgia, Maj. Hezekiah Bussey

28th Georgia, Capt. John A. Johnson

ARTILLERY
DEPARTMENT OF SOUTHERN VIRGINIA AND NORTH CAROLINA

Col. Hilary Polard Jones

Branch's Battalion

Maj. James C. Coit

Halifax (Virginia) Battery, Capt. Samuel T. Wright

Petersburg (Virginia) Battery, Capt. Richard G. Pegram

FURTHER READING

Andrews, J. Cutler. The South Reports the Civil War. Princeton,
   NJ: Princeton University Press, 1970. Andrews's work is a
   compilation of contemporary accounts of the Southern
   aspects of the Civil War.

Beringer, Richard E., et al. Why the South Lost the Civil War.
   Athens: University of Georgia Press, 1986. The authors dis-
   cuss various viewpoints concerning the reasons for
   Confederate defeat.

Berlin, Ira, ed. Freedom: A Documentary History of
   Emancipation1861–1867, Series 2: The Black Military
   Experience. Cambridge: Cambridge University Press, 1982.
   Berlin presents a compilation of contemporary letters, dis-
   patches and documents concerning black troops in the Civil
   War.

Bernard, George S. "The Battle of the Crater, July 30, 1864."
   In Southern Historical Society Papers, vol. 18., 3–38
   Richmond: Virginia Historical Society, 1890. Bernard's is a
   first-person, Southern account of the battle.

Bernard, George S. "Great Battle of the Crater." Southern
   Historical Society Papers, vol.28, 204–221. Richmond:
   Virginia Historical Society, 1900.

Bradford, Ned, ed. Battles and Leaders of the Civil War. New
   York: Appleton Century Crofts, 1956. A well-chosen collection of accounts by participants of the war.

Brock, Robert A., ed. Southern Historical Society Papers, vol. 28,
   307–308.

Richmond: Southern Historical Society, 1900. The Papers provide firsthand but at times long after the event recollections of the war from a southern viewpoint.

Catton, Bruce. Glory Road. Garden City, NJ: Doubleday, 1952.
   Though not trained as a historian, Catton provides a well-
   written and well-researched account of the Army of the
   Potomac.

Cavanaugh, Michael Arthur, and William Marvel. The Petersburg Campaign: The Battle of the Crater: "The Horrid Pit," June 25–August 6, 1864. Lynchburg, VA: H.E. Howard, 1989. "The Horrid Pit" is one of the best, most focused and researched accounts of the Battle of the Crater. It was of incalculable help in researching this book.

Clark, George. "Alabamians in the Crater Battle," Confederate Veteran, Vol. III, 1895, 68–70. Clark's article is a first-person reminiscence of the battle.

Coffin, Charles Carleton. Four Years of Fighting: A Volume of Personal Observation with the Army and Navy, From the First Battle of Bull Run to the Fall of Richmond. Boston: Tickner and Fields, 1866. Coffin's contemporary accounts of the war are from a decidedly Northern perspective and are often inaccurate.

Davis, William C. Death in the Trenches. Alexandria: Time-Life Books, 1986. Davis's book, part of the Time-Life "The Civil War" series, is well illustrated and highly readable.

_____. The Image of War 1861–1865, vol 6: The End of an Era. Garden City, NJ: Doubleday, 1984. Davis couples well-written narrative with an excellent collection of contemporary photographs.

Day, W.A. "Battle of the Crater," Confederate Veteran, Vol. XI, 1903, 355–356. Day's account, although written years later, provides first-hand accounts of the battle.

Featherston, John C. "Graphic Account of Battle of Crater," In Southern Historical Society Papers, vol. 33, 358–374. Richmond: Virginia Historical Society, 1905. Featherston's is a lively first-person Southern account of the battle.

_____. "Incidents of the Battle of the Crater," Confederate Veteran, Vol. XIV, 1906, 23–26. Featherston relates Southern accounts of the battle.

Foote, Shelby. The Civil War: A Narrative, Red River to Appomattox. New York: Random House, 1974. Shelby Foote is known for his very readable style.

Frassanito, William A. Grant and Lee: The Virginia Campaigns. New York: Scribner's, 1983. Frassanito augments his text with an interesting analysis of contemporary photographs compared with modern photographs of the same locale.

Glatthar, Joseph T. Forged in Battle: The Civil War Alliance of Black Soldier and White Officers. New York: The Free Press, 1990. Glatthar offers a well-researched study of the black soldiers' experience in the war.

Grant, U.S. Personal Memoirs of U.S. Grant. New York: Charles L. Webster and Company, 1885. Grant's recollections of his war experiences are classic accounts of the war from the perspective of its most important Union general.

Griess, Thomas E., ed. The American Civil War, The West Point Military History Series. Wayne, NJ: Avery Publishing Group, Inc., 1987. Produced by the West Point History Department, The American Civil War is well-written and well-researched, and contains very useful illustrations.

Houghton, Brevet Major Charles H. "In the Crater." In Battles and Leaders of the Civil War, vol. 4, 561–562. edited by Robert Underwood Johnson and Clarence Clough Buel. New York: Thomas Yoseloff, Inc., 1956. Houghton's is a vivid account by a Union officer who took part in the fighting in the Crater.

Lord, Francis A. They Fought for the Union. New York: Bonanza Books, 1960. An established Civil War historian, Dr. Lord provides a wealth of details concerning the every-day life of Union troops.

Marvel, William. Burnside. Chapel Hill: The University of North Carolina Press, 1991. Marvel's is a very readable, sympathetic biography of the unfortunate general.

Sifakis, Stewart. Who Was Who in the Civil War. New York: Facts on File, 1988. Contains concise biographies and often portraits of important Civil War figures.

Thomas, Henry Goddard. "The Colored Troops at Petersburg."
In Battles and Leaders of the Civil War, vol. 4, 563–567.
edited by Ned Bradford. New York: Appleton Century Crofts,
1956.
_____. "The Colored Troops at Petersburg." In The Tragedy of
the Crater, edited by Henry J. Pleasants, Jr. Boston: The
Christopher Publishing House, 1938. Thomas, a participant
in the battle, provides a vivid, first-hand account in
Pleasants's compilation.
Trudeau, Noah Andre. The Last Citadel: Petersburg, Virginia,
June 1864–April 1865. Boston: Little, Brown, 1991. A well-
written, day-by-day account of the siege of Petersburg. It
offers one of the best-researched accounts of the
Petersburg Campaign and was very helpful in the prepara-
tion of this book.
United States War Department. The War of the Rebellion:
Official Records of the Union and Confederate Armies.
Series 1, vol. 1, part 1. Washington: Government Printing
Office, 1892. Detailed official accounts and reports of the
Civil War submitted by the appropriate participants.
United States Congress, Joint Committee on the Conduct of the
War. Report on the Conduct of the War. Vols. 2–4, 38th
Congress, 20th Session. Washington, 1865. A contemporary
investigation of the various aspects of the war.
Walls, H.H. "Diary." In To Bear Arms, edited by Zeb D.
Harrington and Martha Harrington. Moncure, NC: Zeb D.
and Martha Harrington, 1984. Excerpts of H. H. Walls's
diary were reprinted in the Apex (North Carolina)
Newspaper shortly after the war and were later included in
To Bear Arms, a compilation of Civil War letters and diary
entries.
Warner, Ezra J. Generals in Blue: Lives of the Union
Commanders. Baton Rouge: Louisiana State University
Press, 1964. Along with its companion volume, Generals in
Gray, Warner's book provides concise, accurate biographies
of Civil War generals.

Wheeler, Richard. The Siege of Vicksburg. New York: Thomas Y. Crowell Co., 1978. Wheeler's book details the siege of the ill-fated Mississippi city and provides information concerning an early unsuccessful Union mining operation.

PHOTO CREDITS

We acknowledge the cooperation of the United States Army Military History Institute, Carlisle Barracks, Pennsylvania, for photographs of William F. Bartlett, Simon G. Griffin, Bushrod R. Johnson, James H. Ledlie, William Mahone, Elisha G. Marshall, Henry Pleasants, Robert B. Potter, David A. Weisiger, Orlando B. Willcox, a burial detail at Cold Harbor, a view of Petersberg, Confederate cannon at Petersburg, defensive works at Fort Sedgewick, Cheváux-de-frise, soldiers digging the tunnel, Confederate counter-mine, soldiers carrying powder to the mine, explosion of the mine, Confederate dead, dead artilleryman, cemetery at City Point, the crater after the battle, the crater after the war. Once again we thank Mr. Jim Enos for his assistance.

We acknowledge the Library of Congress for photographs of Ambrose E. Burnside, Edward Ferrero, and George G. Meade.

The drawing of Federal sharpshooters at Petersburg was reproduced from Frank Leslie's Illustrated Newspaper.

The photograph of John A. Flemming was reproduced through the courtesy of the North Carolina Division of Archives and History.

INDEX